Write ONE SkillsBook

Writing Skills Practice

. . . a resource of student activities
to accompany the *Write One* handbook

WRITE SOURCE.

GREAT SOURCE EDUCATION GROUP
a Houghton Mifflin Company
Wilmington, Massachusetts

About the SkillsBook...

The *Write One SkillsBook* is a place to learn and to write. There are three sections in the SkillsBook. The first section focuses on skills and rules to help children grow as writers. The second section is a place to write—everything from journal entries to stories to poems. The final section is a place to put new words in ABC order. This may be a good place to begin.

Trademarks and trade names are shown in this book strictly for illustrative purposes and are the property of their respective owners. The authors' references herein should not be regarded as affecting their validity.

Copyright © 2002 by Great Source Education Group, Inc. All rights reserved.

No part of this work may be reproduced or transmitted in any form or by any means, electronic or mechanical, including photocopying and recording, or by any information storage or retrieval system without the prior written permission of Great Source Education Group unless such copying is expressly permitted by federal copyright law. Address inquiries to Permissions, Great Source Education Group, Inc., 181 Ballardvale Street, Wilmington, MA 01887.

Great Source and **Write Source** are registered trademarks of Houghton Mifflin Company.

Printed in the United States of America

International Standard Book Number: 0-669-49016-4 (student edition)

   2 3 4 5 6 7 8 9 10 -BA- 05 04 03 02

International Standard Book Number: 0-669-49017-2 (teacher's edition)

   1 2 3 4 5 6 7 8 9 10 -BA- 05 04 03 02 01

We hope you will have fun writing!

This SkillsBook belongs to

_____

Table of Contents

Guided Writing Skills 2
Writing Practice 58
A Personal Word Dictionary 86

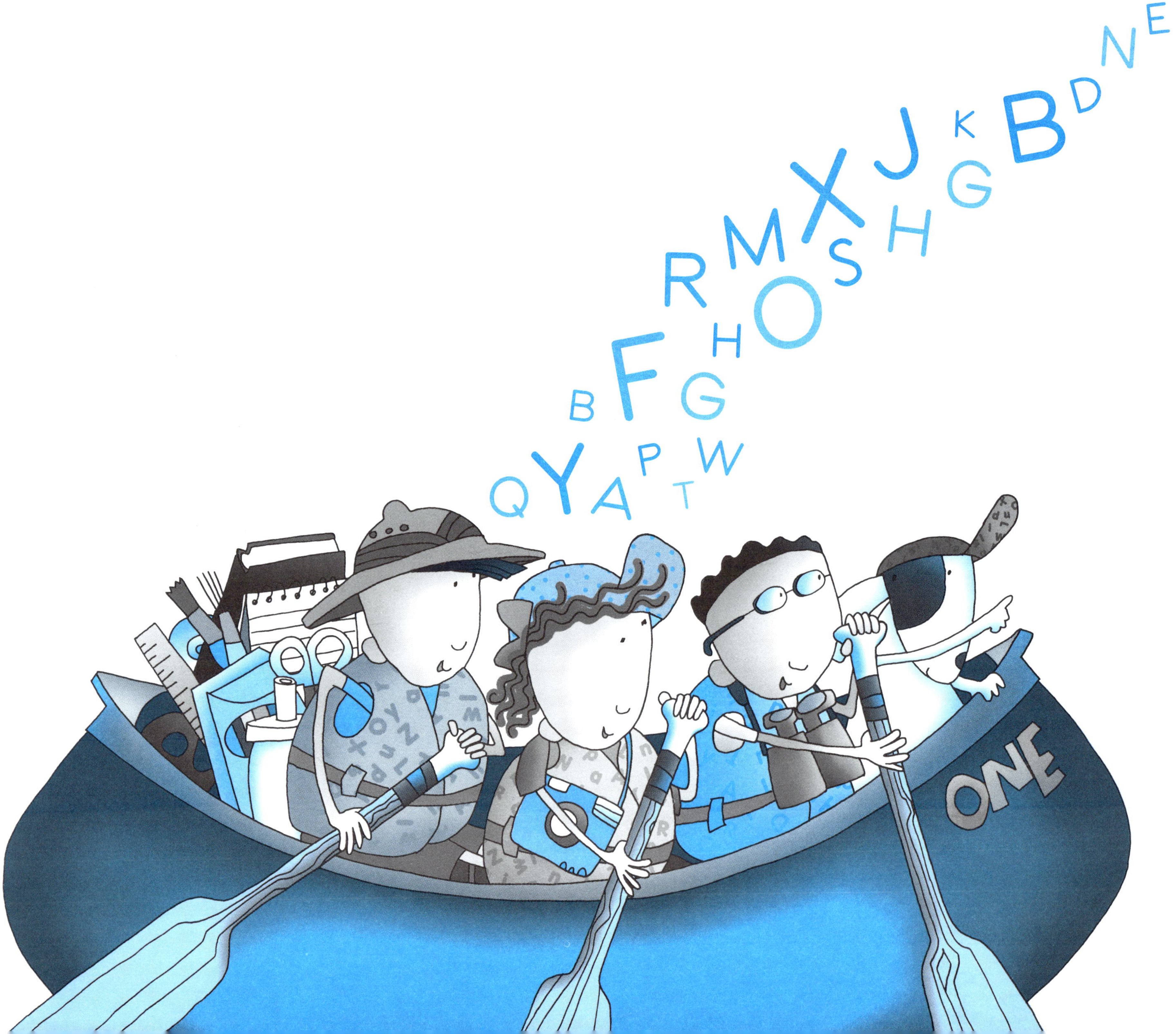
ONE

Guided Writing Skills

Writing Sentences	4	Quotation Marks	34
Telling Sentences	6	Nouns	36
Asking Sentences	8	Proper Nouns	38
Exciting Sentences	10	Pronouns	40
More Sentences	12	More Nouns and Pronouns	42
Capital Letters	14	Verbs	44
More Capital Letters	16	Adjectives	46
Capital Letters Review	18	Nouns, Verbs, and Adjectives	48
Plurals	20	ABC Order	50
More Plurals	22	Everyday Word Sort	52
Periods	24	Using the Right Word 1	54
End Punctuation	26	Using the Right Word 2	56
Commas	28		
Commas in Letters	30		
Apostrophes in Contractions	32		

Writing Sentences

Follow the three sentence rules.

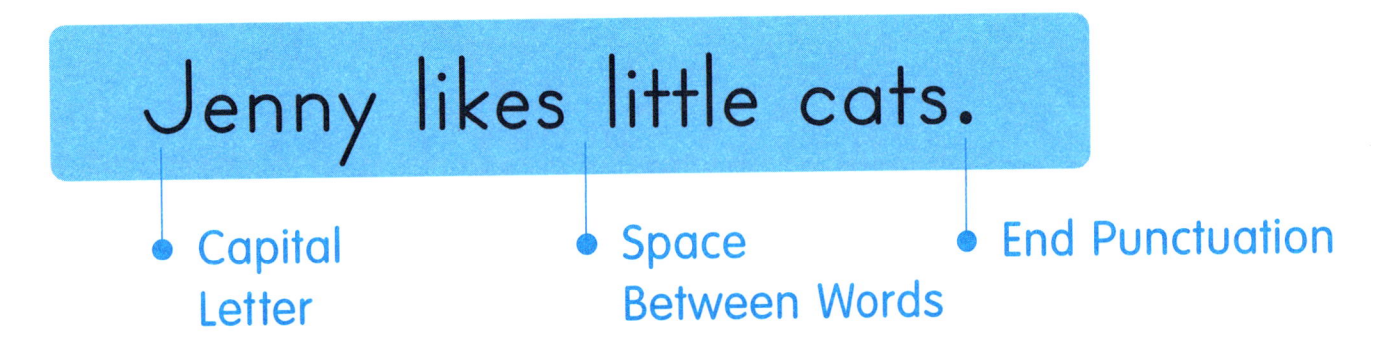

> Jenny likes little cats.

- Capital Letter
- Space Between Words
- End Punctuation

Trace these sentences. See how they follow the sentence rules.

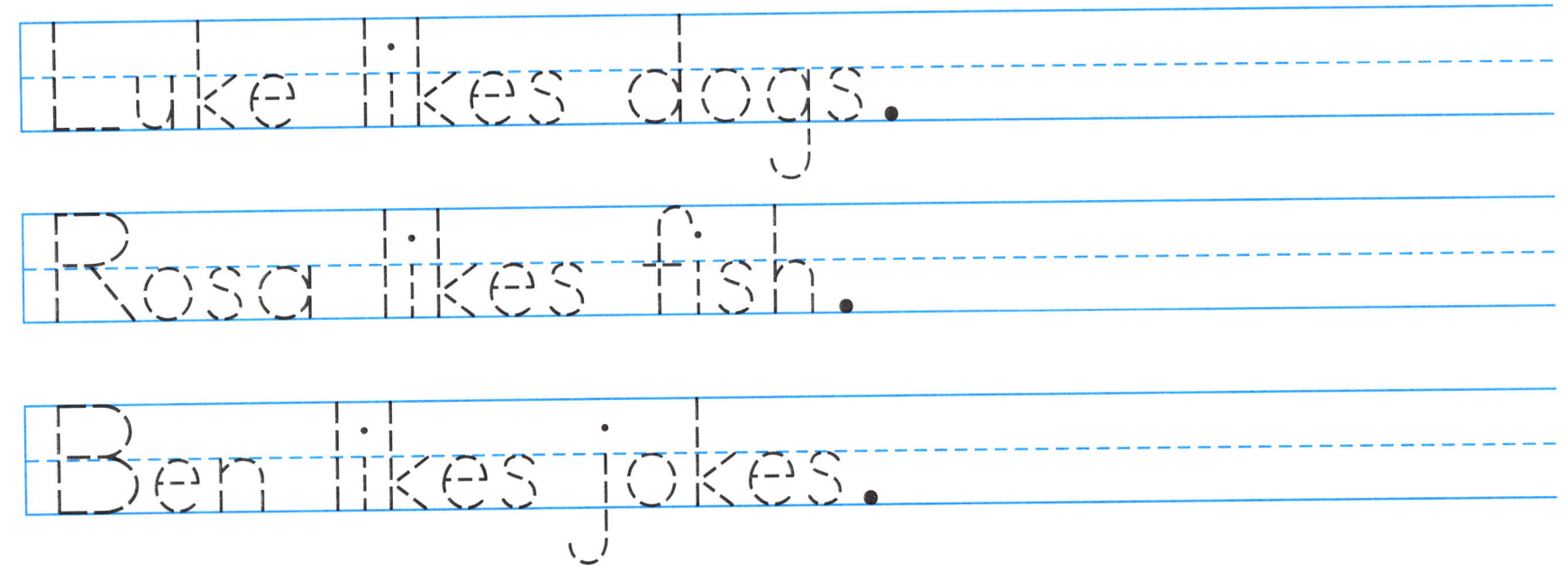

Luke likes dogs.

Rosa likes fish.

Ben likes jokes.

© Great Source. All rights reserved.

Write three sentences about things you like.
Follow the three sentence rules.

Sample: I like ladybugs.

1. I like

2. I like

3. I like

© Great Source. All rights reserved.

6

Telling Sentences

Add more pictures and words to this page. Color the pictures.

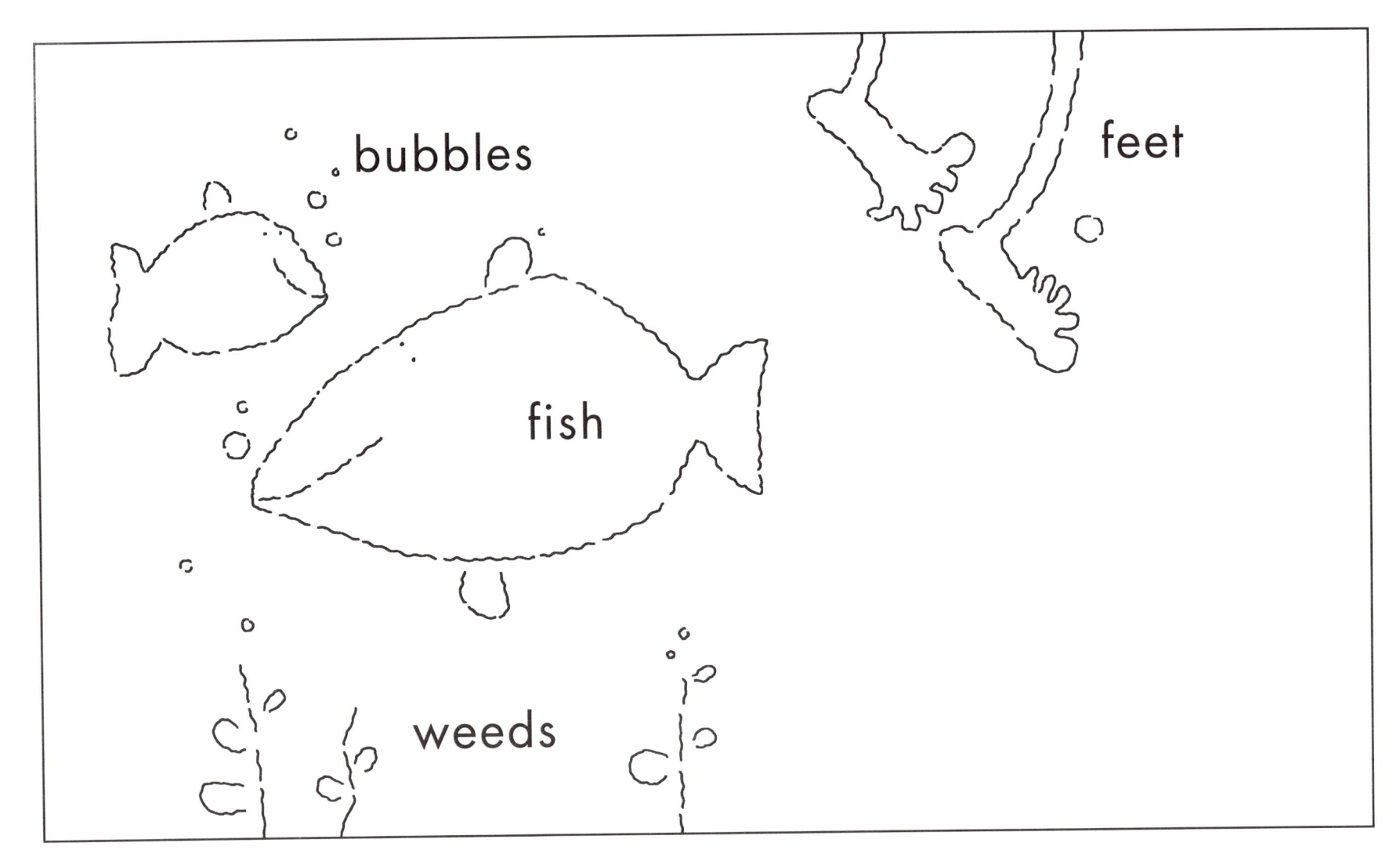

bubbles

feet

fish

weeds

Write three telling sentences about things you see on page 6.

Sample: I see fish.

1. I see

2. I see

3. I see

Asking Sentences

✏ Answer each question below with one of these words.

| mouse   moon   mother   morning |

1. Who is drinking milk?

2. What is another word for "mom"?

3. When does the sun come up?

4. Where does light come from at night?

Finish the asking sentences. Use **mouse** and a question mark **?**.

Sample: Where is the mouse?

1. Who saw the _____

2. What color is the _____

3. When did you see the _____

4. Why do we have a _____

© Great Source. All rights reserved.

Exciting Sentences

Write a weather word for each picture.

> rainy   sunny   windy   snowy

1.

2.

3.

4.

Finish each exciting sentence with a different weather word from page 10. Add an exclamation point !.

Sample: Wow, it's cold!

1. Wow, it's _____

2. Wow, it's _____

3. Wow, it's _____

4. Wow, it's _____

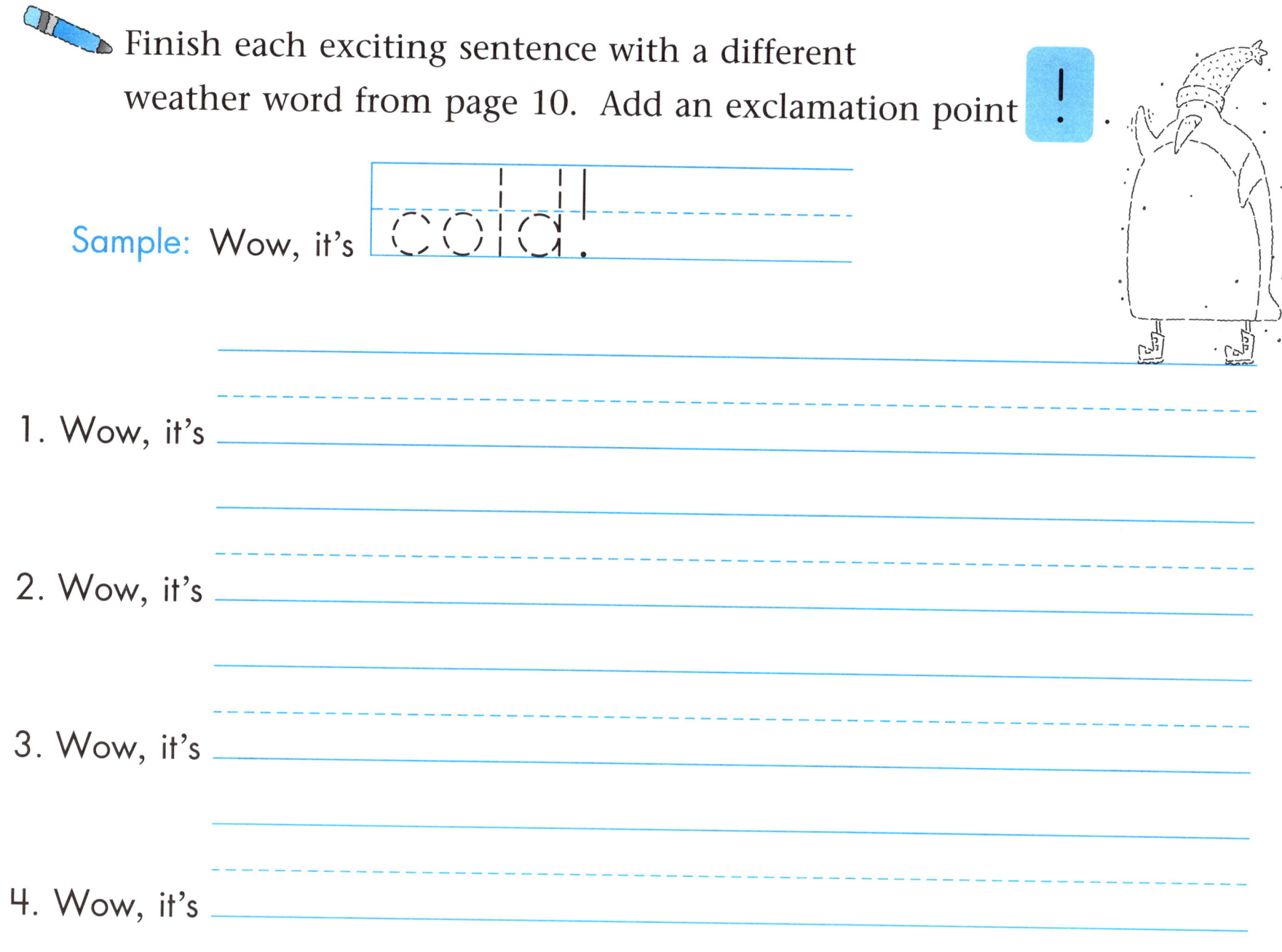

© Great Source. All rights reserved.

More Sentences

✏️ Write two telling sentences about yourself.

_____

_____

✏️ Write two asking sentences beginning with the word where .

_____

_____

✏️ Write two exciting sentences about a storm.

✏️ Write two funny sentences.

Capital Letters

Draw a picture of yourself and a friend. Then write your first names.

Answer these questions with words that begin with capital letters.

1. What is your name?

2. What is your school's name?

3. Which is your birthday month? (Look at a calendar.)

4. Where do you live (state)? (Look at a map.)

More Capital Letters

Copy these sentences. Use capital letters at the beginning of each sentence. Use capital letters for special names.

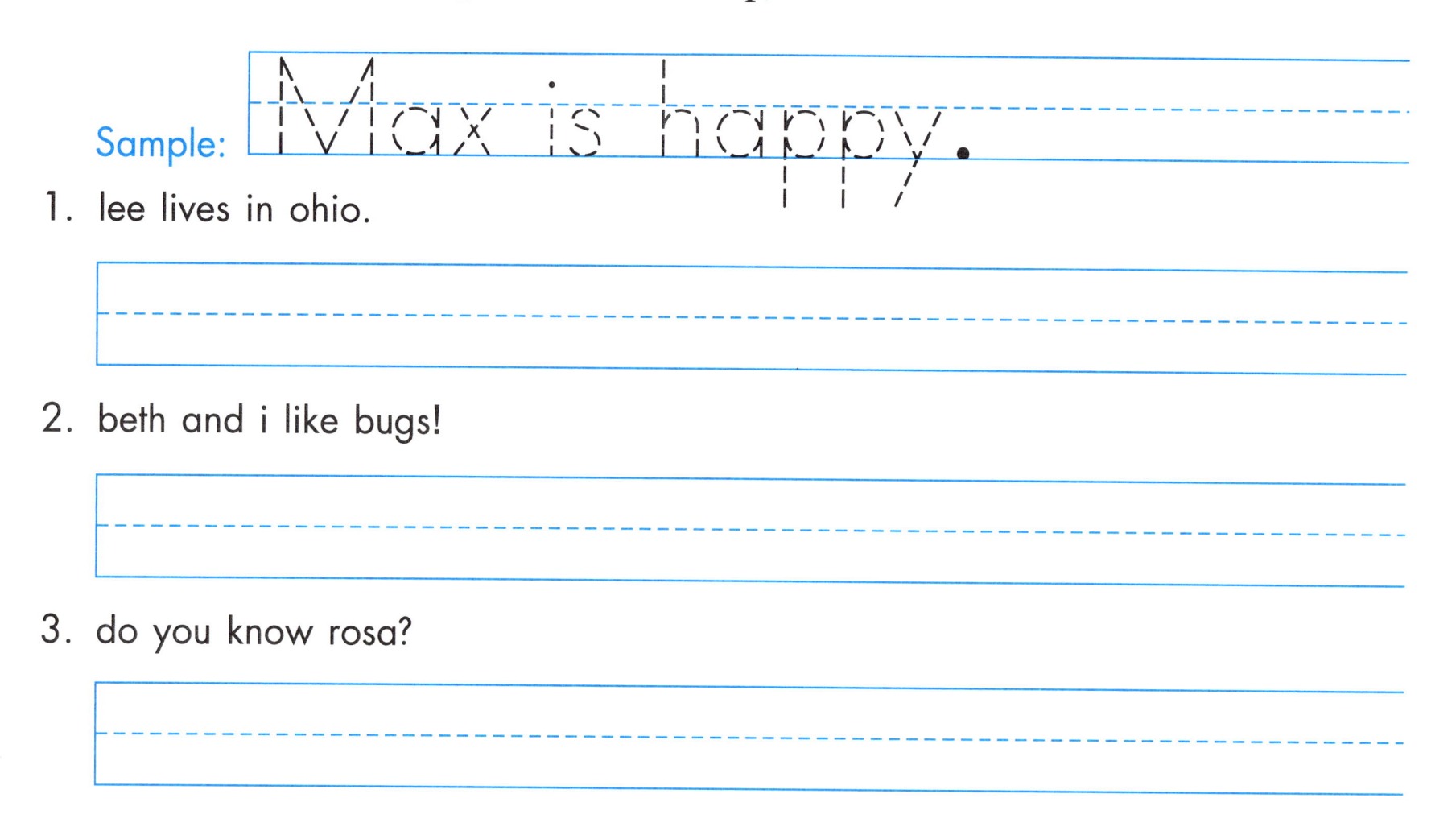

Sample: Max is happy.

1. lee lives in ohio.

2. beth and i like bugs!

3. do you know rosa?

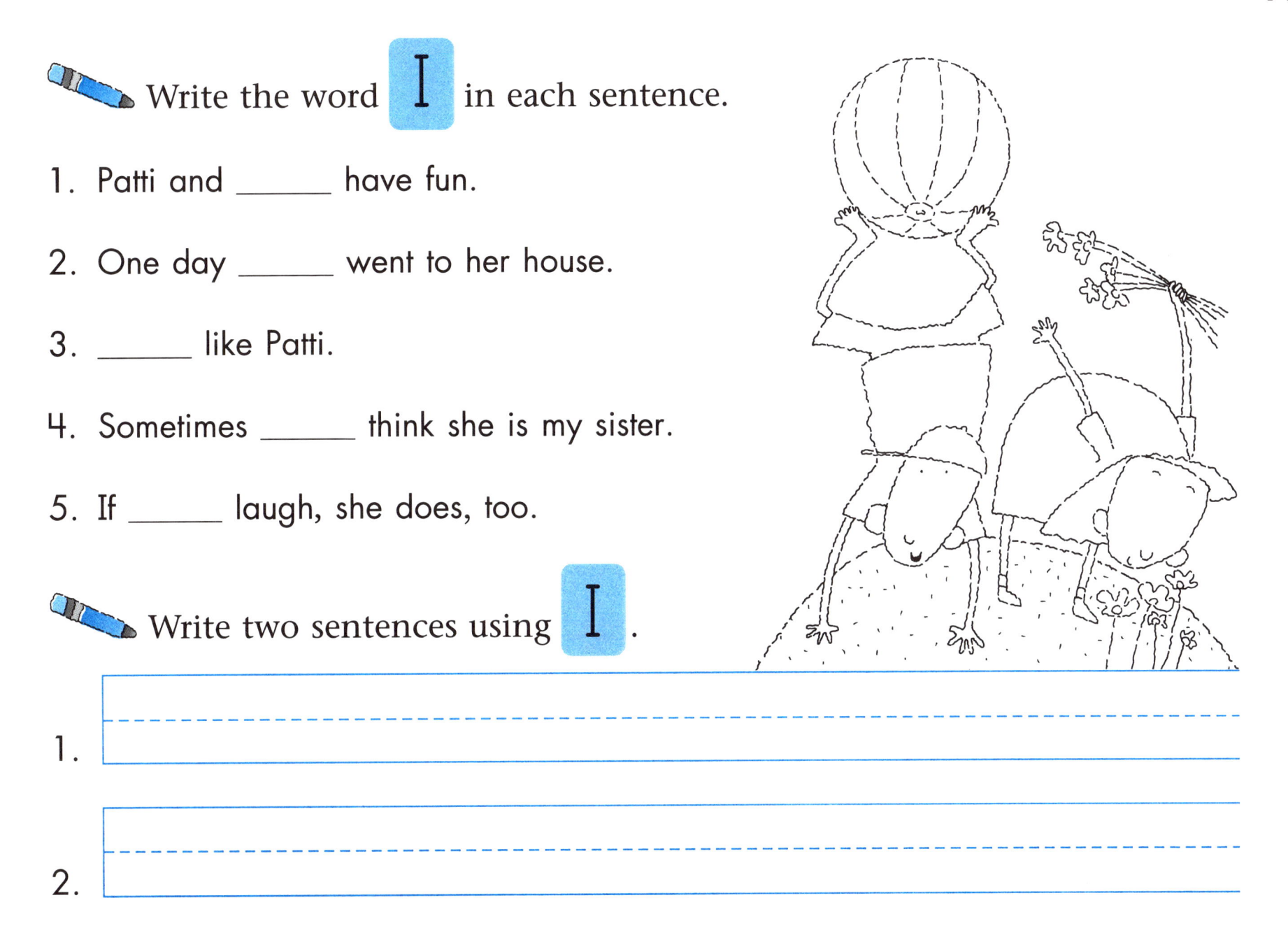

✏️ Write the word **I** in each sentence.

1. Patti and _____ have fun.

2. One day _____ went to her house.

3. _____ like Patti.

4. Sometimes _____ think she is my sister.

5. If _____ laugh, she does, too.

✏️ Write two sentences using **I**.

1. _____

2. _____

Capital Letters Review

Copy these sentences. Use capital letters where you need them.

1. may i have some milk?

2. it is time for lunch.

3. jackson lives in utah.

4. dad and i ride bikes.

✏️ Write the first names of four classmates.

1. _____   3. _____

2. _____   4. _____

✏️ Write the names of four special places.
Use the maps in your handbook.

1. _____   3. _____

2. _____   4. _____

Plurals

Make plurals by adding **s** to these animal names.

1. duck — ducks
2. bear
3. bat
4. cat
5. chick
6. lion
7. seal
8. frog
9. horse
10. parrot

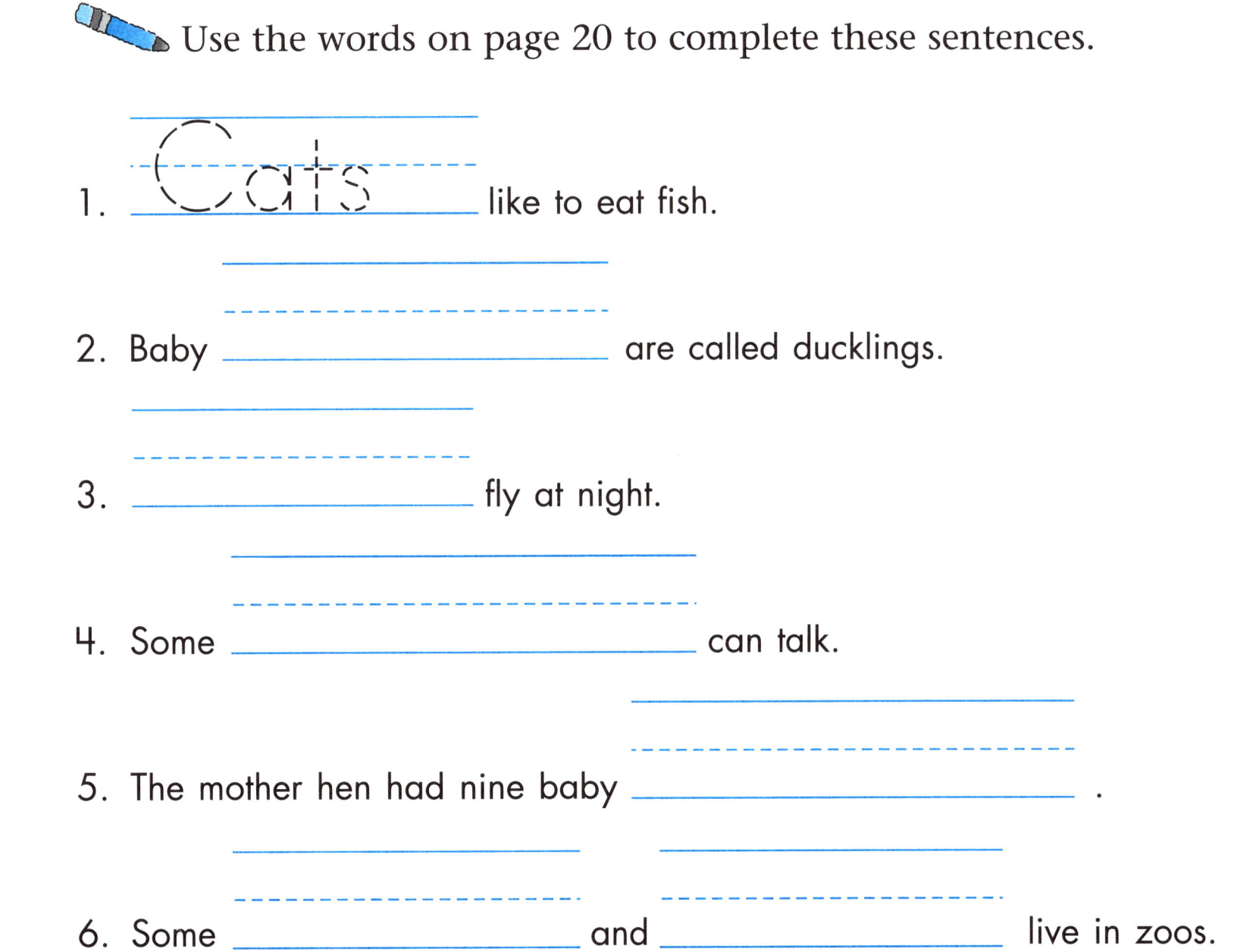

Use the words on page 20 to complete these sentences.

1. __Cats__ like to eat fish.

2. Baby _____ are called ducklings.

3. _____ fly at night.

4. Some _____ can talk.

5. The mother hen had nine baby _____ .

6. Some _____ and _____ live in zoos.

© Great Source. All rights reserved.

More Plurals

Write a word for each picture.

hats   bugs   rings   balls   turtles   flowers

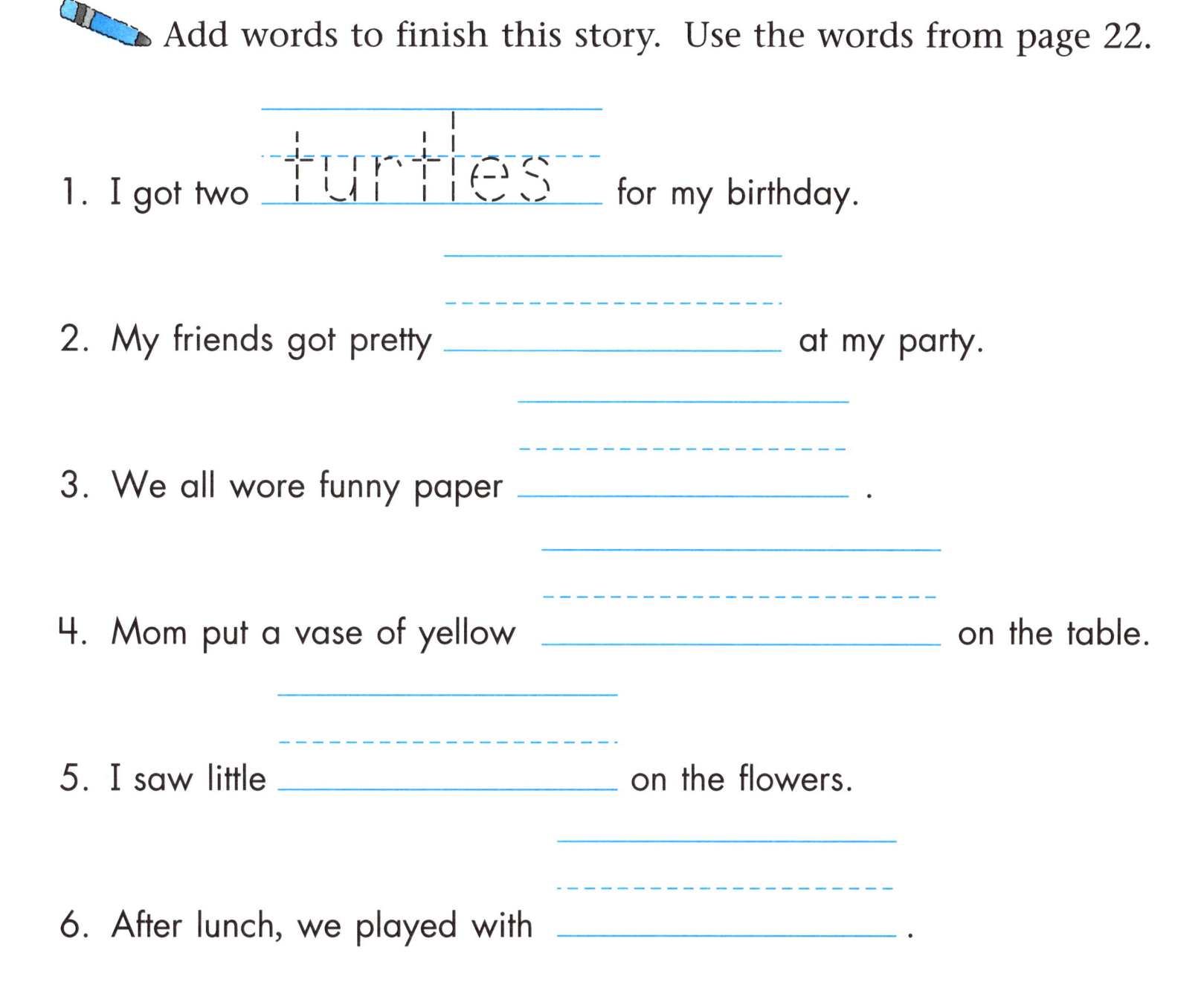

Add words to finish this story. Use the words from page 22.

1. I got two ___turtles___ for my birthday.

2. My friends got pretty _____ at my party.

3. We all wore funny paper _____ .

4. Mom put a vase of yellow _____ on the table.

5. I saw little _____ on the flowers.

6. After lunch, we played with _____ .

© Great Source. All rights reserved.

Periods

Add a day of the week to each sentence. Put a period . at the end. Use a calendar to find the days.

1. Today is _____

2. Yesterday was _____

3. Tomorrow is _____

4. I like _____

5. My busy day is _____

Add a period [.] to each abbreviation.

1. Mrs____ Lopez bakes a cake.

2. Ms____ Lee helps Mrs____ Lopez.

3. Dr____ Tran likes the frosting.

4. Mr____ Cook washes the pans.

Draw a picture about the sentences.

End Punctuation

Add end punctuation to each sentence . ? !.

1. Pat and Max are friends____

2. What do Pat and Max do____

3. They fly kites____

4. Sometimes they tell jokes____

5. They laugh and laugh____

6. Where do they live____

7. They live in Florida____

8. Yippee____

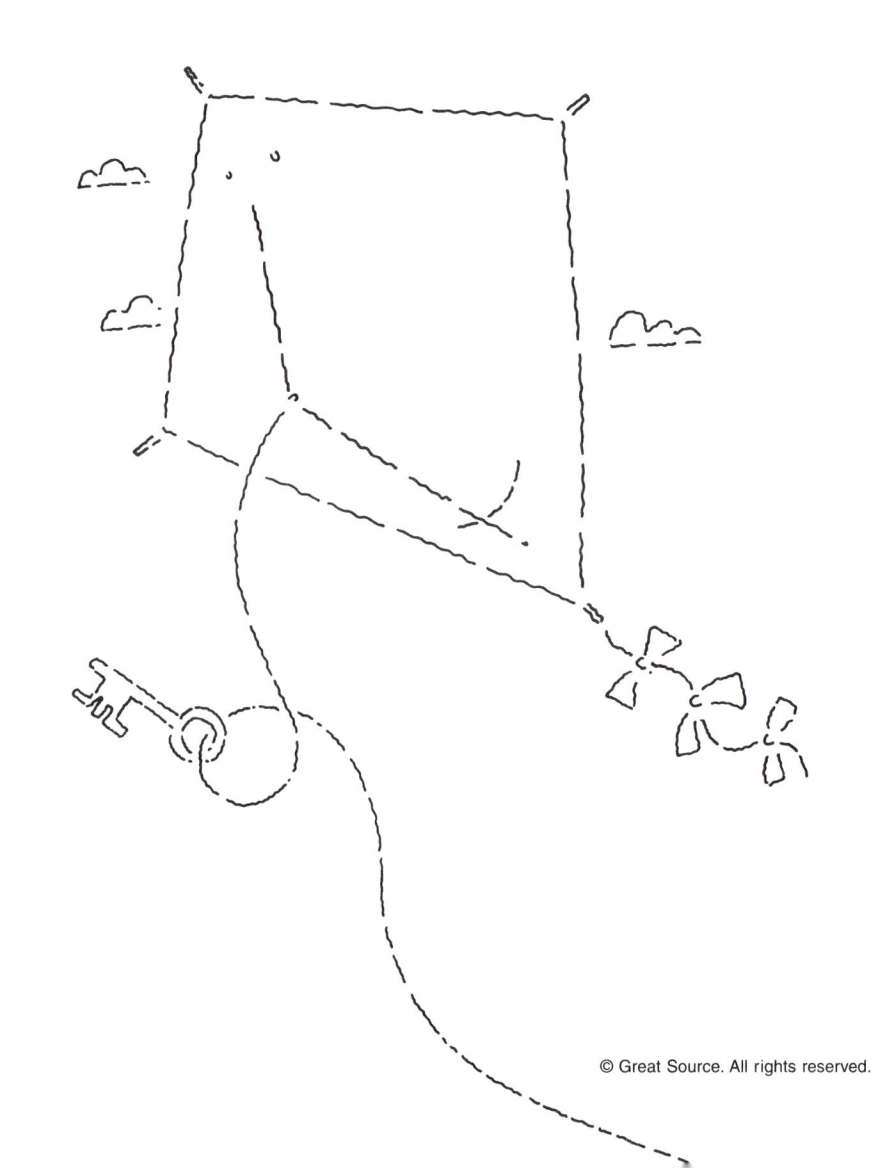

Add a punctuation mark . ? ! to each sentence. Then answer each riddle. Use the words on handbook page 184.

1. I am very big____
   I have a long trunk____
   What am I____

2. I live in the ocean____
   I have eight legs____
   What am I____

3. I am black and white____
   I make a bad smell____
   What am I____

4. I am a big cat____
   I like to roar____
   What am I____

Handbook Pages 126–127, 130–131, and 184

28

Commas

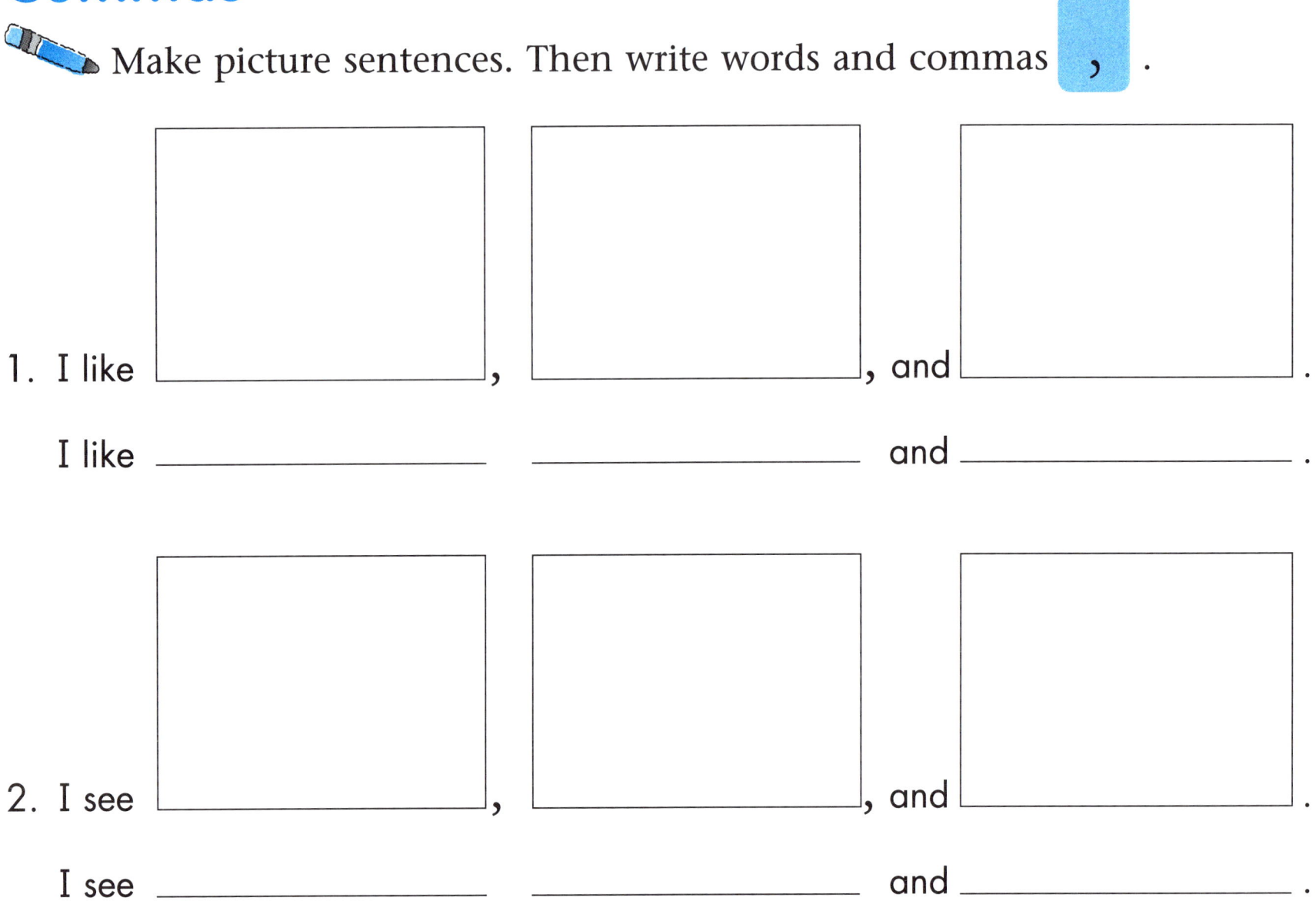

Make picture sentences. Then write words and commas **,** .

1. I like ☐ , ☐ , and ☐ .

   I like _____ _____ and _____ .

2. I see ☐ , ☐ , and ☐ .

   I see _____ _____ and _____ .

© Great Source. All rights reserved.

Write four answers below. Put commas (,) where they belong.

1. This is today's date.

2. I live in this city and state.

3. These are the three colors of the American flag.

4. This is the greeting I would write in a letter to my friend.

© Great Source. All rights reserved.

Commas in Letters

Trace the commas (,) in this letter.

> August 2, 2002
>
> Dear Tom,
>
>   Bring your checkers to school. We can play at recess. It will be fun.
>
>   See you soon,
> Sara

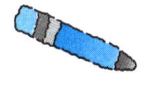

Write a short letter. Use commas **,** where they belong.

Date _____

Greeting _____

Message
_____
_____
_____
_____

Closing _____

Your name _____

31

Apostrophes in Contractions

Draw a line between the words and their contractions.

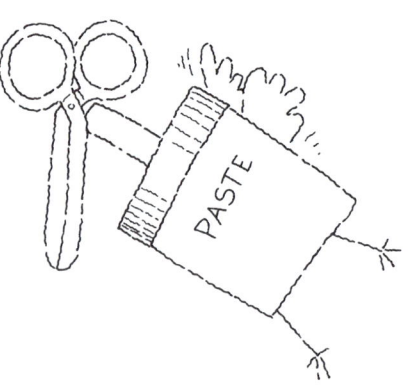

Two Words	Contractions		Two Words	Contractions
1. are not	isn't		6. we have	I'll
2. is not	don't		7. I will	you're
3. did not	aren't		8. it is	we've
4. do not	didn't		9. you are	we're
5. I am	I'm		10. we are	it's

Write the two words for each contraction.

1. We're having fun.   We are

2. It's a sunny day.

3. I'm riding my bike.

4. You're roller-skating.

5. I don't have skates.

6. I'll ride slowly.

Quotation Marks

Put quotation marks around a speaker's words.

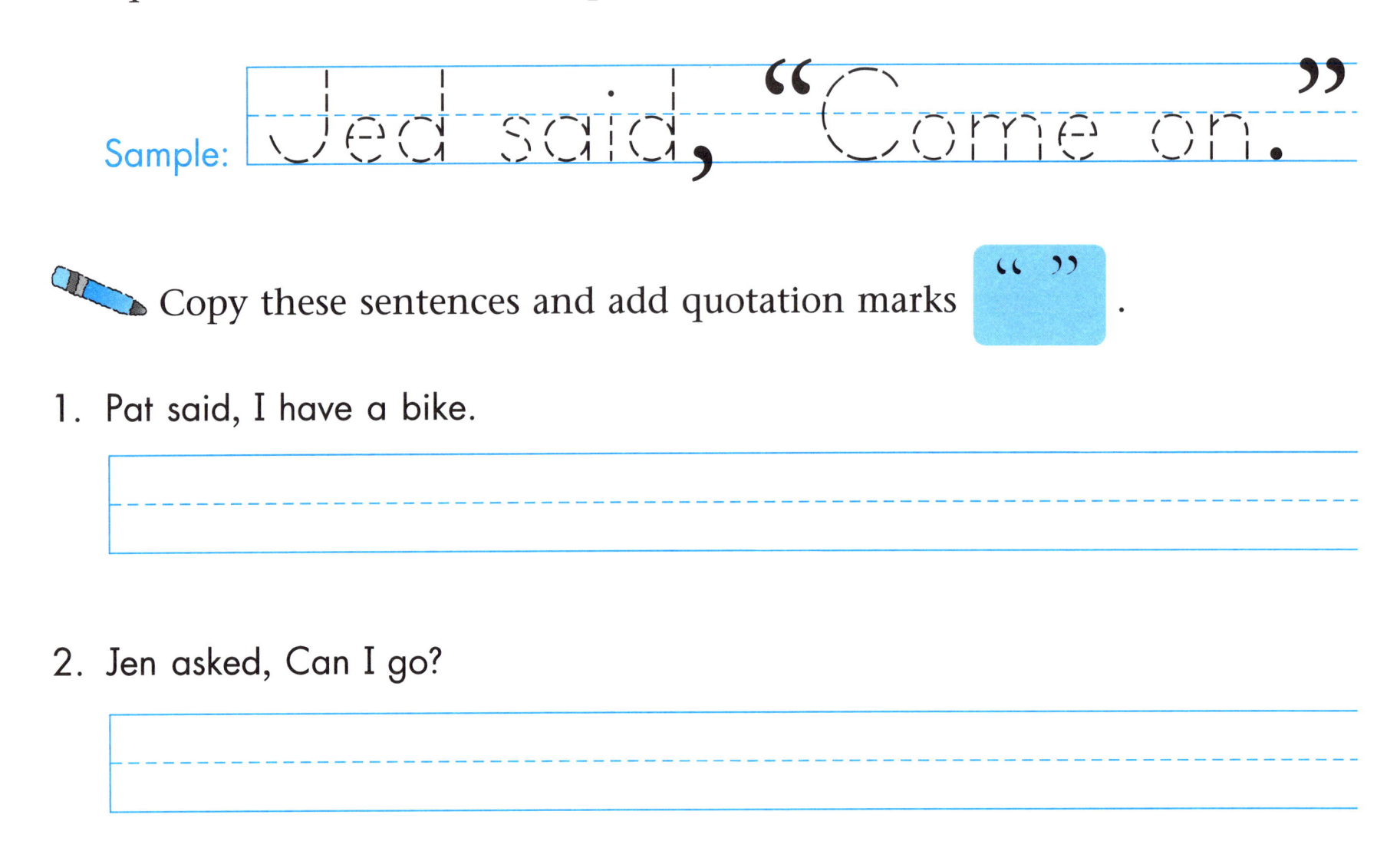

Sample: Jed said, "Come on."

Copy these sentences and add quotation marks " ".

1. Pat said, I have a bike.

2. Jen asked, Can I go?

Quotation Marks

Use quotation marks to say these kind things.

> Good morning   Pardon me   Please

Sample: I say, "Thank you."

1. I say,

2. I say,

3. I say,

Nouns

Look in your handbook to find names of people, places, and things.

1. Write the names of two people.

2. Write the names of two places.

3. Write the names of two things.

Use one of your nouns in a sentence.

Add these nouns to the story.

> peanuts   water   noses   hose
> mouths   hands   food

Long Noses

Elephants have long ____noses____ called trunks. They use them to

put _____ and _____ into their _____ .

Trunks also spray water like a _____ . Elephants use their trunks like

_____ . They pick up _____ and leaves.

Proper Nouns

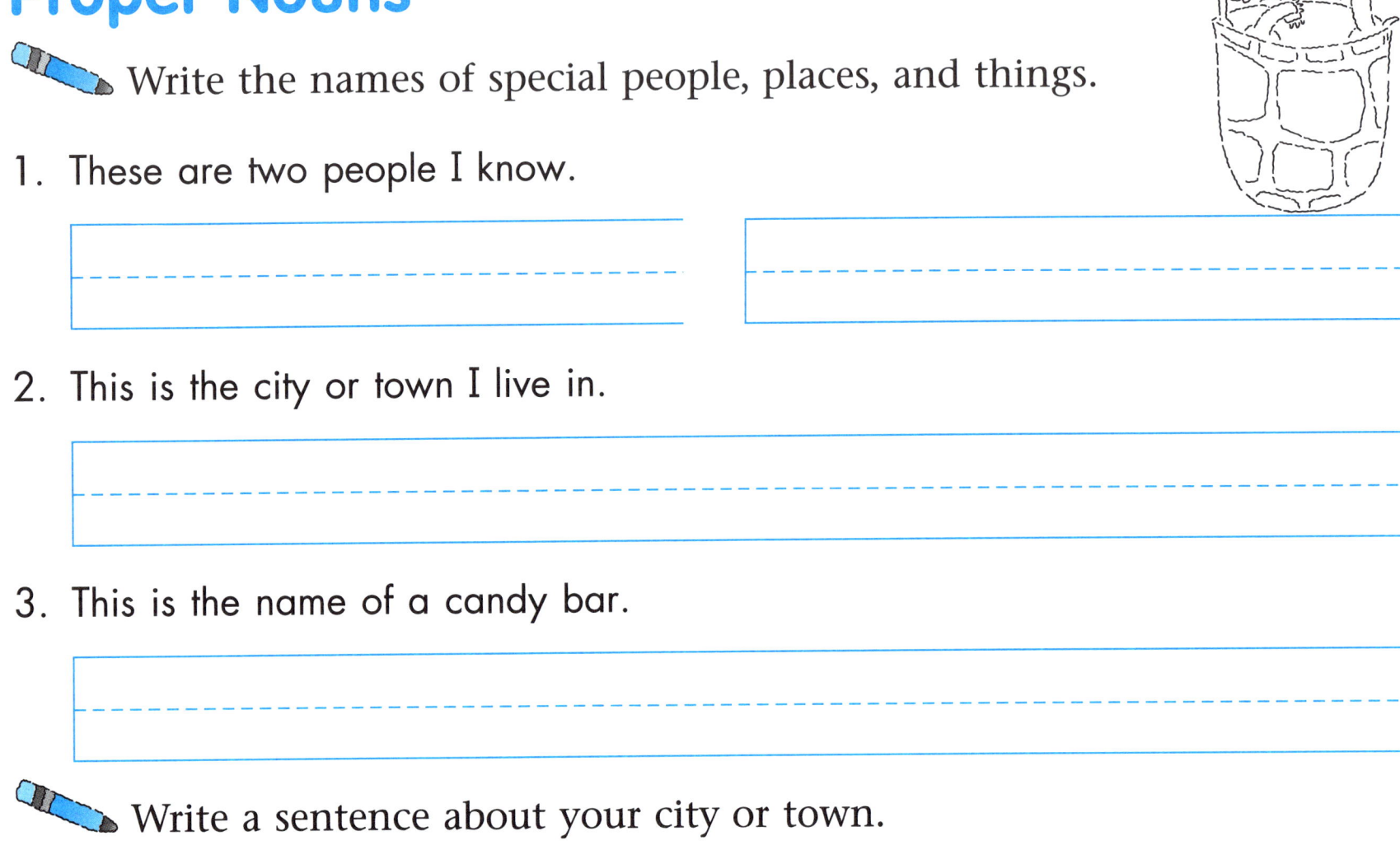

✏️ Write the names of special people, places, and things.

1. These are two people I know.

   _____   _____

2. This is the city or town I live in.

   _____

3. This is the name of a candy bar.

   _____

✏️ Write a sentence about your city or town.

_____

Draw a picture or add photos of your family. Write the names beside their pictures.

Pronouns

Rewrite the sentences. Use one of these pronouns for the underlined words.

They   He   her

1. I saw <u>Sally</u> at the park.

2. <u>Sam</u> was with Sally.

3. <u>Sam and Sally</u> had popcorn.

Choose one pronoun to finish each sentence.

1. I me — Mom, Dad, and _____ have a garden.
2. we us — Working in the garden is fun for_____.
3. me I — Dad helps _____.
4. He Him — _____ digs holes.
5. I Me — _____ plant seeds.
6. She We — _____ water the garden.
7. it they — The sun shines on _____.
8. it they — Sometimes _____ rains.
9. we us — Soon _____ will see plants.

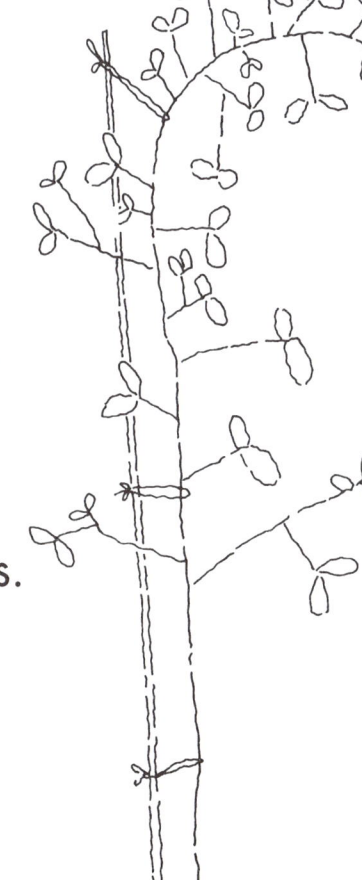

© Great Source. All rights reserved.

More Nouns and Pronouns

List these words in the correct columns.

home   father   Beth   car   school
Ohio   wagon   clown   tape

1. Persons

2. Places

3. Things

Add these pronouns to the sentences.

I it you me

1. _____ lost my hat.

2. Did _____ find _____ ?

3. Please give _____ to _____ .

4. Where was _____ ?

5. Thank _____ .

Draw your hat.

43

Verbs

Add one of these verbs to each sentence.

> talk　bark　croak　purr
> peep　grunt　buzz　roar

1. Pigs grunt.

2. Dogs _____.

3. Cats _____.

4. Frogs _____.

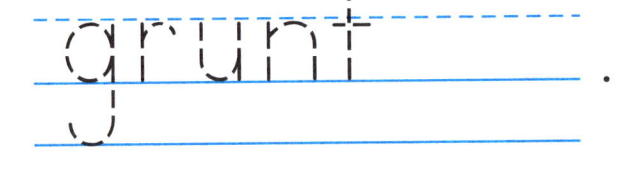

5. Bees _____.

6. Birds _____.

7. Lions _____.

8. People _____.

© Great Source. All rights reserved.

Circle these verbs in the story.

> cooked   washed   picked   ate   drove
> lifted   visited   made   put   peeled

Apple Day

Jake and Dad (visited) an apple farm. They picked some apples and put them in a box. Dad lifted the box into the car. Then they drove home.

After supper Jake washed some apples. Dad peeled them and cooked them on the stove. He made applesauce. Then they ate the applesauce. Yummy!

Adjectives

Write an adjective on each line and draw a picture.

red   green   happy   little   hot   yellow

| _____ turtle | _____ man | _____ sun |
| _____ book | _____ apple | _____ mouse |

© Great Source. All rights reserved.

47

Write a color word under each car. Then color the cars.

1.
2.
3.
4.
5.
6.

© Great Source. All rights reserved.

Nouns, Verbs, and Adjectives

List these words in the correct columns.

> dog   green   hot   rides
> bike   Anna   likes   funny   looks

1. Nouns

2. Verbs

3. Adjectives

© Great Source. All rights reserved.

Write sentences using some of the words on page 48.

Sample: Anna likes the dog.

1.

2.

3.

4.

ABC Order

Write these words in ABC order.

cup   ape   ladybug   ducks   girl   eggs
fish   igloo   jacket   bug   kite   hat

1. ape
2.
3.
4.
5.
6.
7.
8.
9.
10.
11.
12.

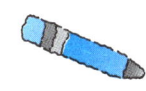

Write these words in ABC order.

milk   owl   x-ray   pet
vase   toy   quilt   soap
nest   wagon rain   us

1. milk
2.
3.
4.
5.
6.
7.
8.
9.
10.
11.
12.

Everyday Word Sort

Write these everyday words in ABC order.

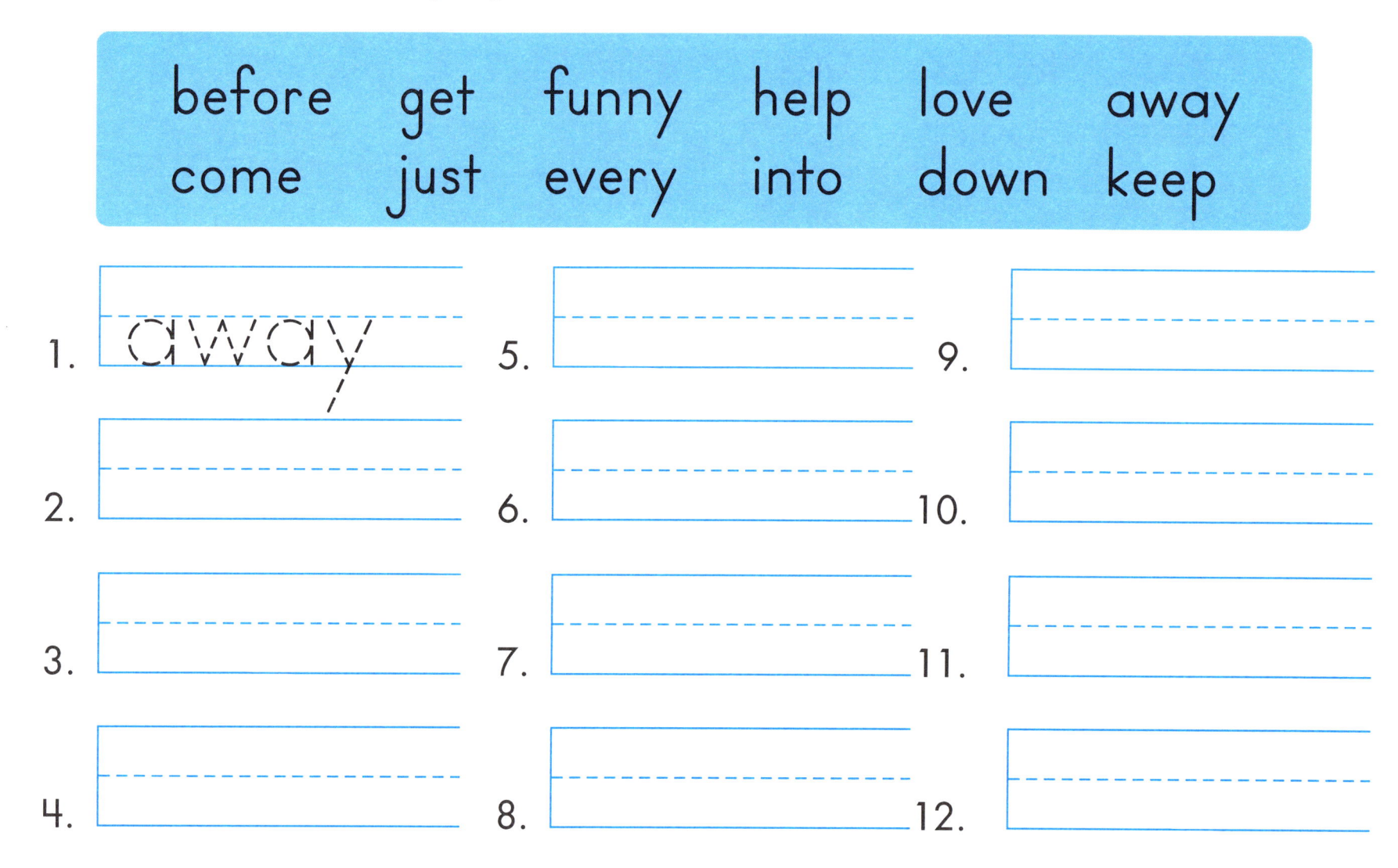

> before   get   funny   help   love   away
> come   just   every   into   down   keep

1. away
2.
3.
4.
5.
6.
7.
8.
9.
10.
11.
12.

Write these words in ABC order.

once	said	put	upon
very	x-ray	more	new
quiet	ride	they	who

1. more
2.
3.
4.
5.
6.
7.
8.
9.
10.
11.
12.

Using the Right Word 1

Write **son** or **sun** on each line.

1. The _____ shines on hot days.

2. Sometimes clouds hide the _____ .

3. Mrs. Lee has a little _____ .

4. Our _____ warms the earth.

5. My uncle has one _____ .

6. The _____ is shining this morning.

7. Wow, look at the _____ going down.

8. Josh is the oldest _____ .

son

sun

© Great Source. All rights reserved.

Write **tail** or **tale** on each line.

1. A lion and a tiger each have a long _____ .

2. A monkey can hang by its _____ .

3. Our class read a silly _____ about a fox.

4. A boxer dog has a short _____ .

5. I like the _____ about the helpful boy.

6. Ms. Moss told a funny _____ .

7. The cat caught its _____ in the door.

8. Our pet pig has a curly _____ .

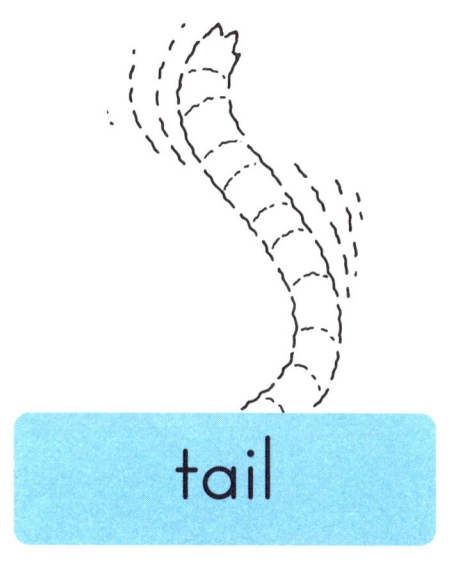

Using the Right Word 2

Trace **to,** **too,** and **two** for each example below.

to

I'm going **to** the store.

too

May I go, **too**?
("Too" means also.)

two

Let's buy **two** toys.
("Two" means 2.)

Use these words to fill in the blanks below.

to   too   two

One day Dee and Ben went _____ the store.

They wanted _____ get _____ birthday presents. They wanted _____ get _____ cards, _____ . They found _____ funny toys. They found _____ funny cards, _____ .

58

Writing Practice

Writing in Journals 60	**Writing a Description** 72
Writing Lists 62	**How-To Writing** 74
Writing Friendly Notes 64	**Writing Captions** 76
Writing Friendly Letters 66	**Writing About Books** 78
Writing a Story About Me 68	**Writing a Story** 80
	Writing Poems 82
Writing About Others 70	**Writing with a Pattern** 84

Writing in Journals

Draw and write on these pages.

Date

Date _____

Writing Lists

Write your own list on this page. Show what you know.

A List About _____
(your topic)

✏️ Have fun writing this list.

Special Words I Like to Say

_____

_____

_____

_____

_____

_____

_____

_____

_____

Writing Friendly Notes

Practice writing notes on these pages.

A Note for Someone Special

A Thank-You Note

Writing Friendly Letters

Write a letter to someone.

Date _____

Greeting _____

Message

_____

_____

_____

_____

Closing _____

Your name _____

© Great Source. All rights reserved.

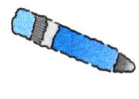

Address this envelope. On envelopes, the U.S. Postal Service wants you to use all capital letters and no punctuation.

Writing a Story About Me

Plan your story about a happy time. Then write it.

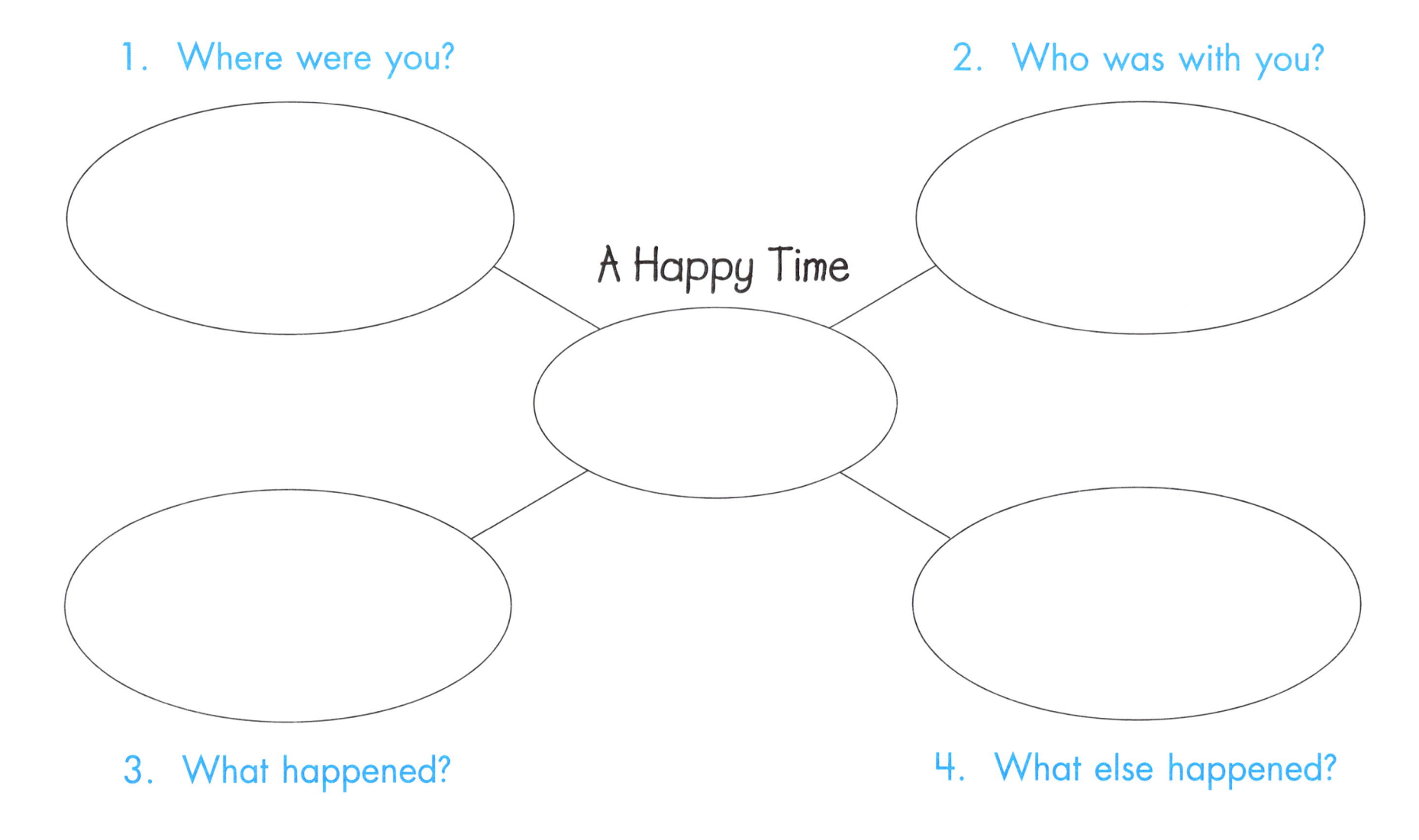

1. Where were you?

2. Who was with you?

A Happy Time

3. What happened?

4. What else happened?

A Happy Time

70

Writing About Others

Attach a photo or draw a picture of a special person. Then write a story about the person.

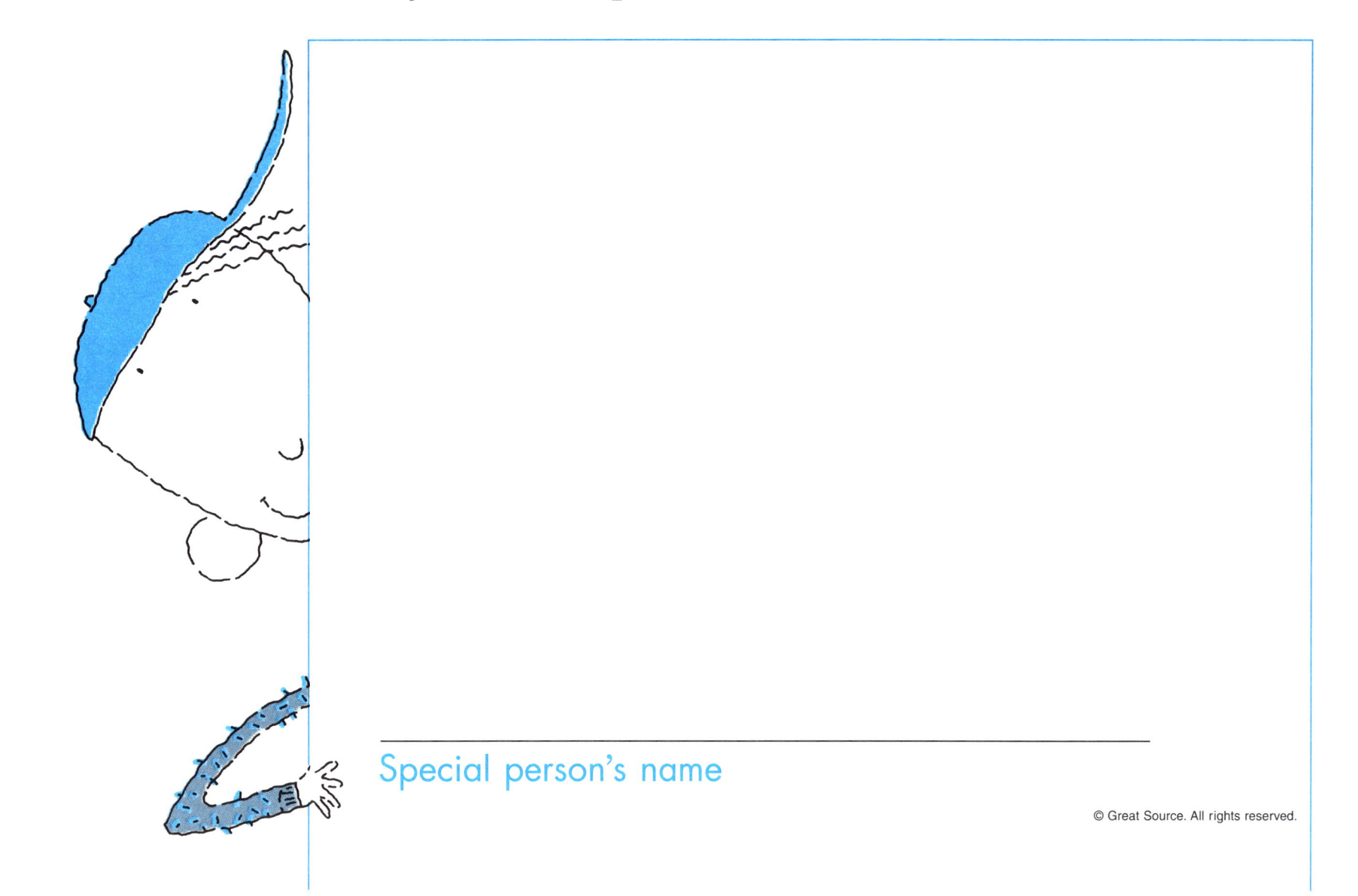

Special person's name

A Special Person

72

Writing a Description

Draw or attach a picture of a person, place, or thing. Then write about your picture.

Use your senses to describe your picture.

How-To Writing

Choose something you know how to do. Draw pictures of the steps you use when you do it.

1.	2.
3.	4.

Now write the steps. (Use the pictures on page 74 to help you.)

1.

2.

3.

4.

Writing Captions

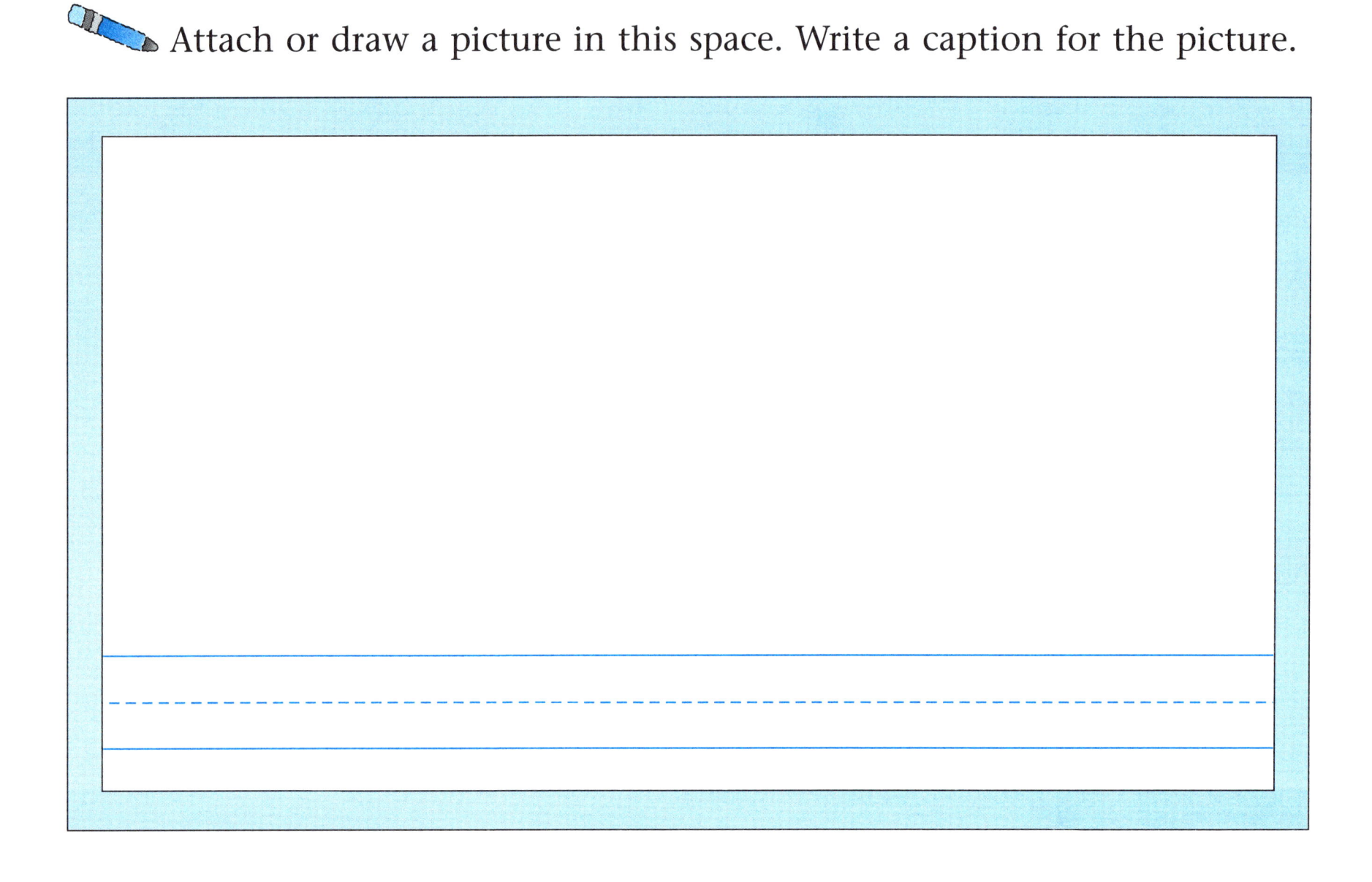

Attach or draw a picture in this space. Write a caption for the picture.

Color this bulletin board. Write a caption for it.

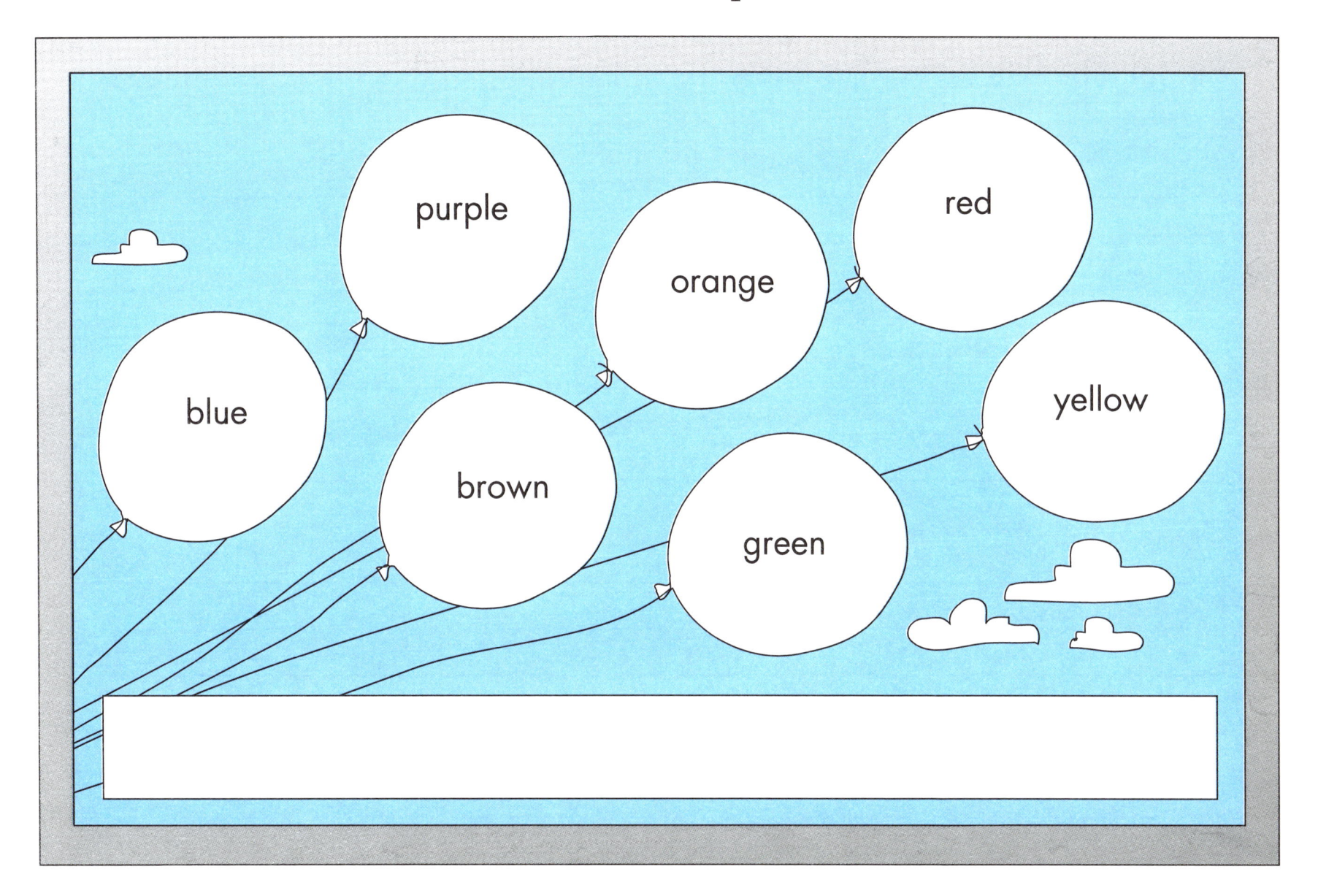

- purple
- red
- orange
- blue
- yellow
- brown
- green

Writing About Books

Tell about a book you like. Fill in the blanks.

1. The name of the book:

2. The book's author:

3. The main character in the book:

4. I like this book because . . .

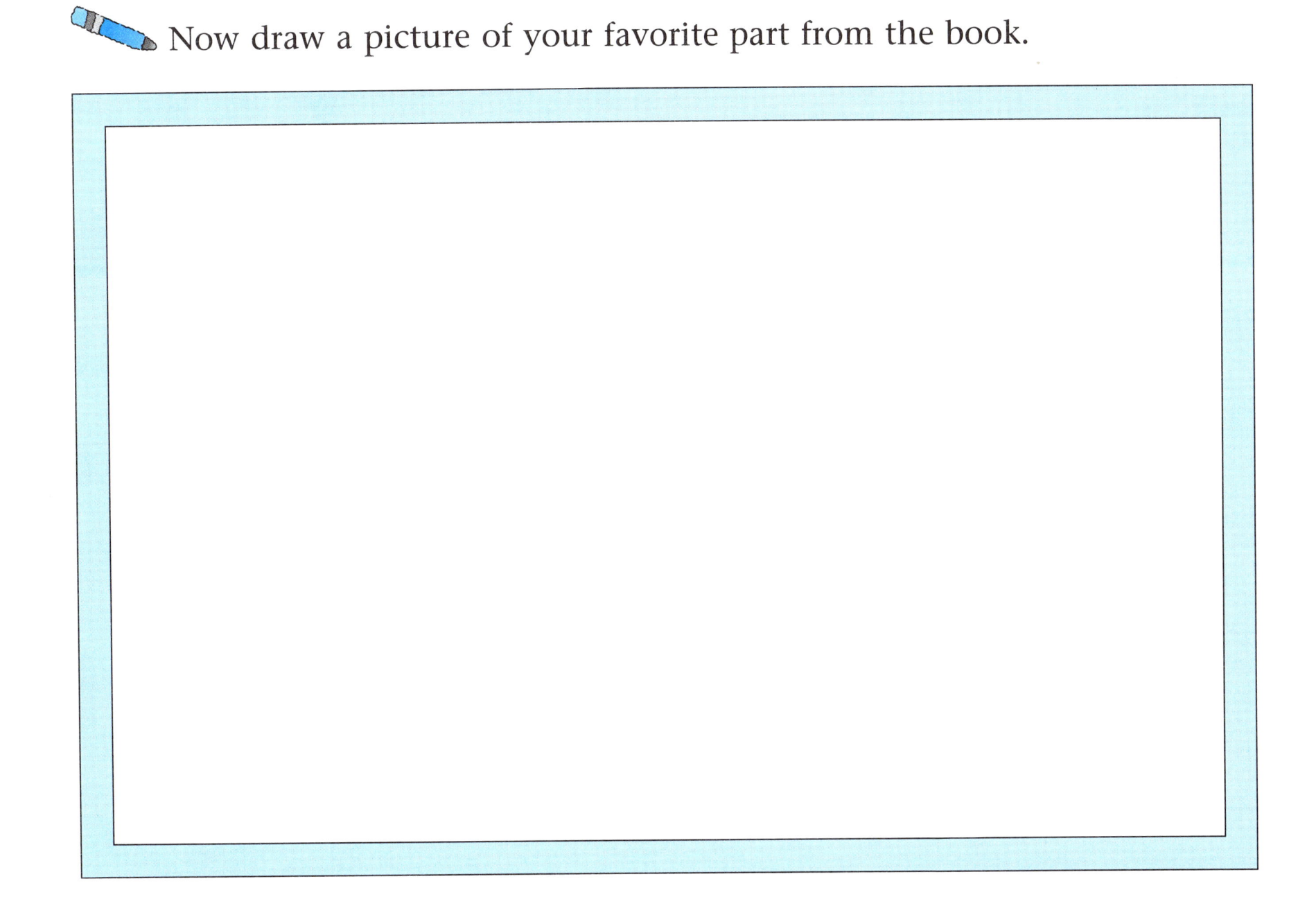

Now draw a picture of your favorite part from the book.

Writing a Story

Draw a picture of a person or an animal doing something. Then write a story to go with your picture.

Be sure your story has a beginning, a middle, and an ending.

Writing Poems

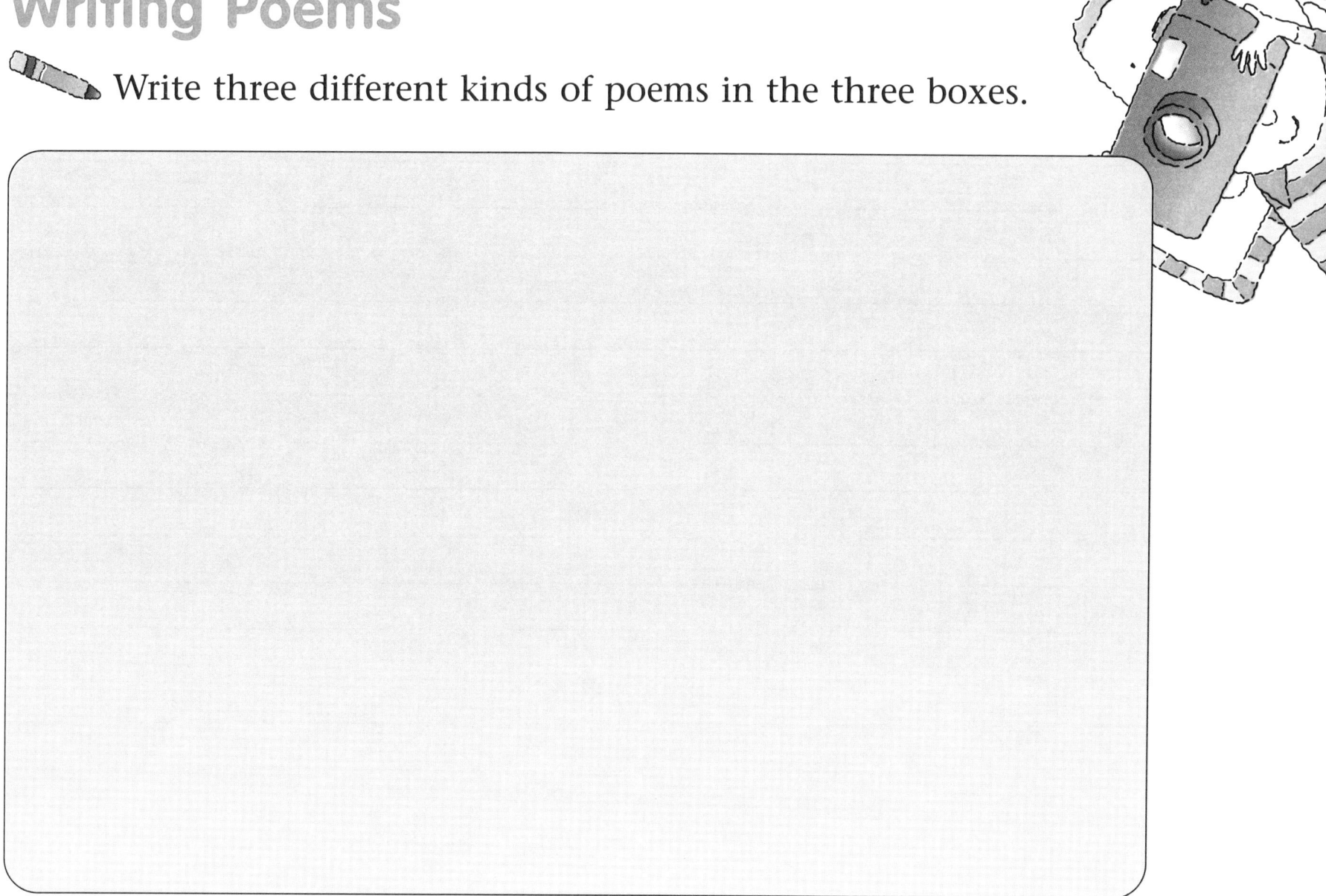

Write three different kinds of poems in the three boxes.

Writing with a Pattern

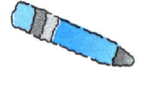

Read the nursery rhyme. Then write your own rhyme, using this pattern.

Hickory, dickory, dock,

The mouse ran up the clock;

The clock struck one,

The mouse ran down,

Hickory, dickory, dock.

New Rhyme for "Hickory Dickory Dock"

Try one of these lines to get started: Lickety, rickety, run or Hickory, dickory, dog.

86

A Personal Word Dictionary

My Words and Pictures

A	88
B	90
C	92
D	94
E	96
F	98
G	100
H	102
I	104
J	106
K	108
L	110
M	112
N	114
O	116
P	118
Q	120
R	122
S	124
T	126
U	128
V	130
W	132
X	134
Y	136
Z	138

Alphabet Poem 140

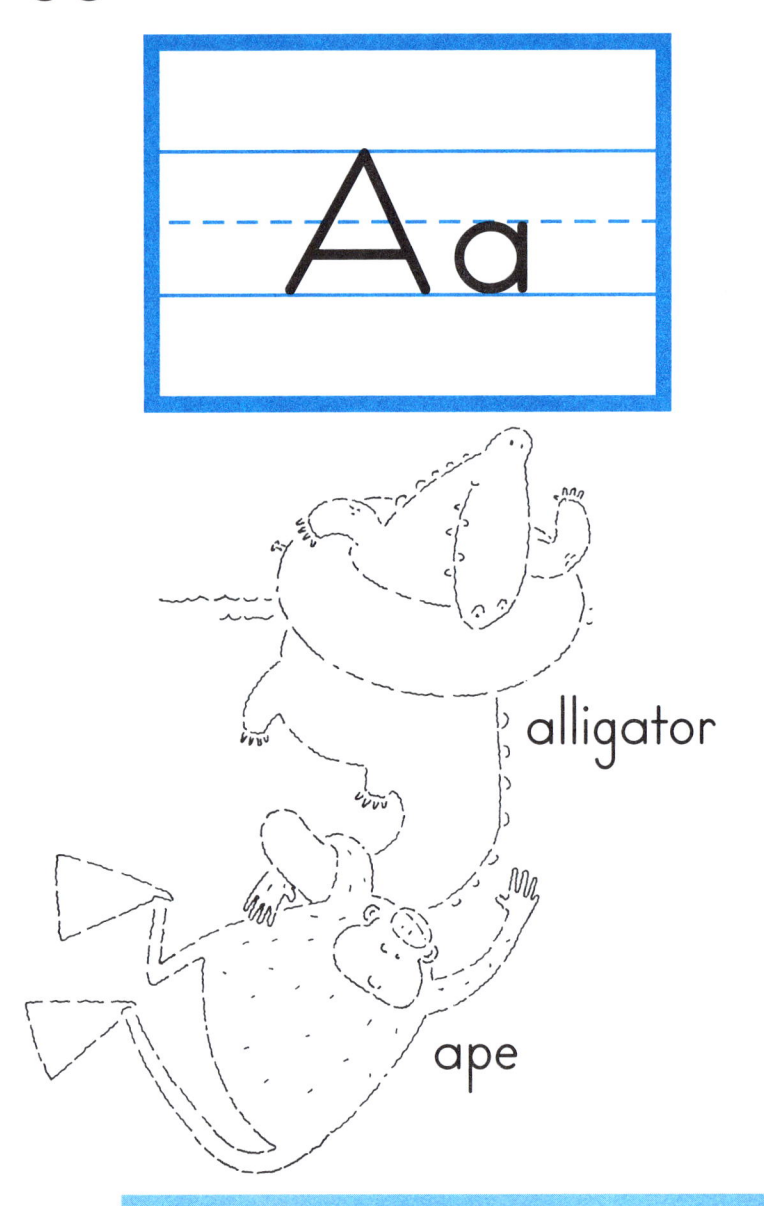

My Words and Pictures

Aa

alligator

ape

Aa Bb Cc Dd Ee Ff Gg Hh Ii Jj Kk Ll Mm Nn Oo Pp Qq Rr Ss Tt Uu Vv Ww Xx Yy Zz

© Great Source. All rights reserved.

about

after

again

My Words and Pictures

Bb

butterfly

bow

Aa Bb Cc Dd Ee Ff Gg Hh Ii Jj Kk Ll Mm Nn Oo Pp Qq Rr Ss Tt Uu Vv Ww Xx Yy Zz

baby

brother

boy

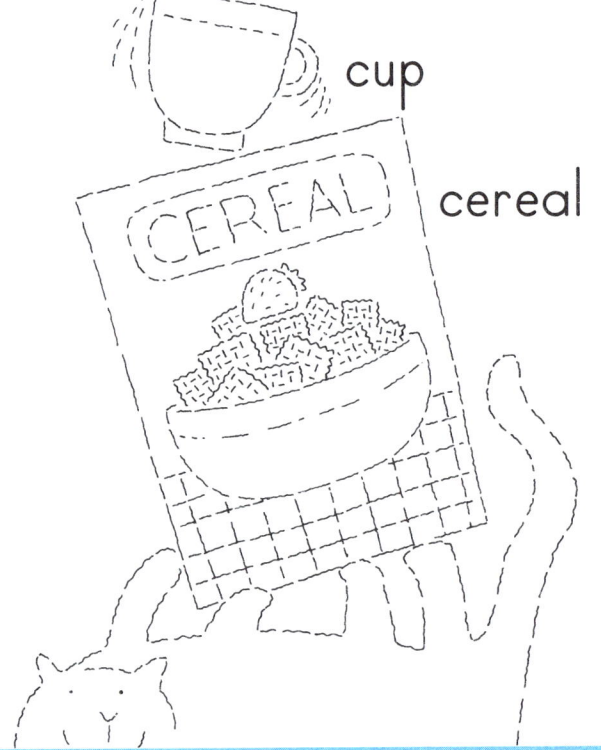

My Words and Pictures

Cc

cup

cereal

Aa Bb Cc Dd Ee Ff Gg Hh Ii Jj Kk Ll Mm Nn Oo Pp Qq Rr Ss Tt Uu Vv Ww Xx Yy Zz

call

car

city

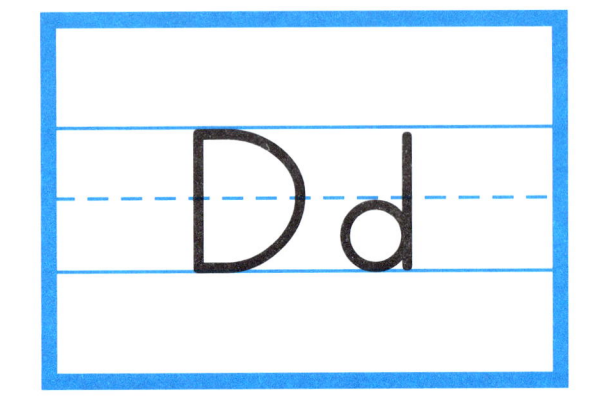

My Words and Pictures

Dd

ducks

Aa Bb Cc Dd Ee Ff Gg Hh Ii Jj Kk Ll Mm Nn Oo Pp Qq Rr Ss Tt Uu Vv Ww Xx Yy Zz

© Great Source. All rights reserved.

daddy

down

dog

96

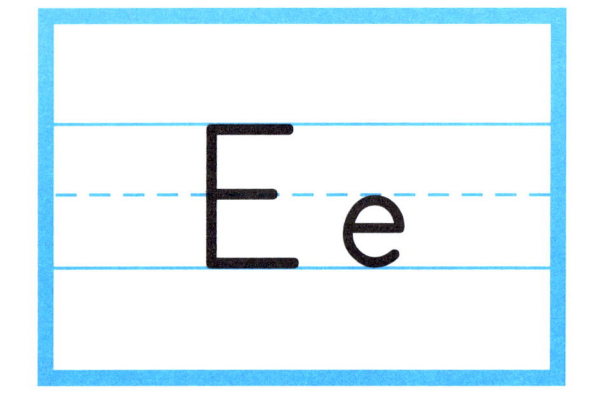

Ee

My Words and Pictures

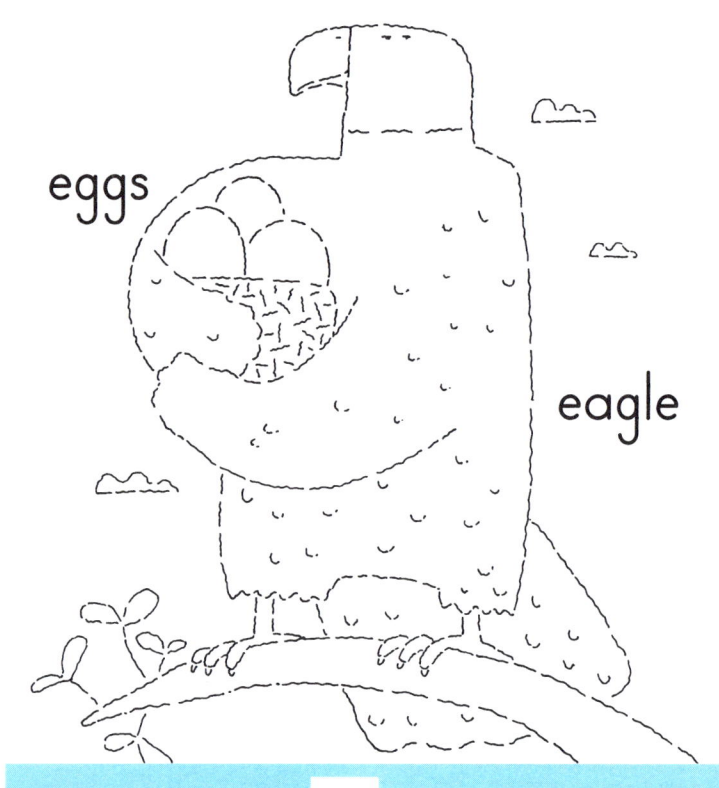

eggs

eagle

Aa Bb Cc Dd Ee Ff Gg Hh Ii Jj Kk Ll Mm Nn Oo Pp Qq Rr Ss Tt Uu Vv Ww Xx Yy Zz

© Great Source. All rights reserved.

eat

each

every

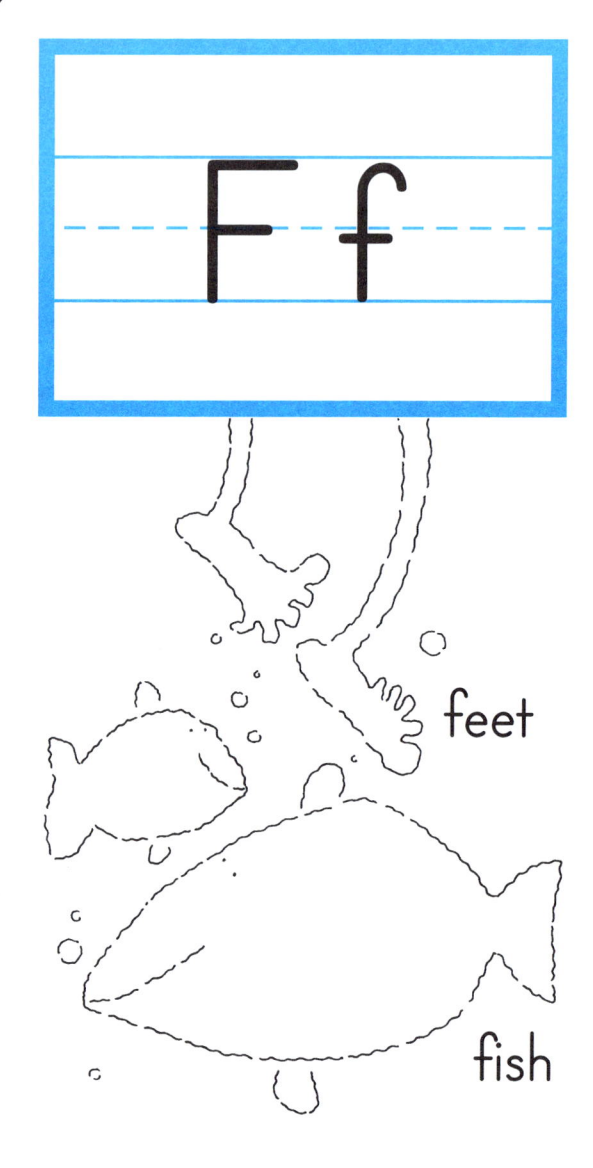

My Words and Pictures

Ff

feet

fish

Aa Bb Cc Dd Ee Ff Gg Hh Ii Jj Kk Ll Mm Nn Oo Pp Qq Rr Ss Tt Uu Vv Ww Xx Yy Zz

© Great Source. All rights reserved.

father

funny

friend

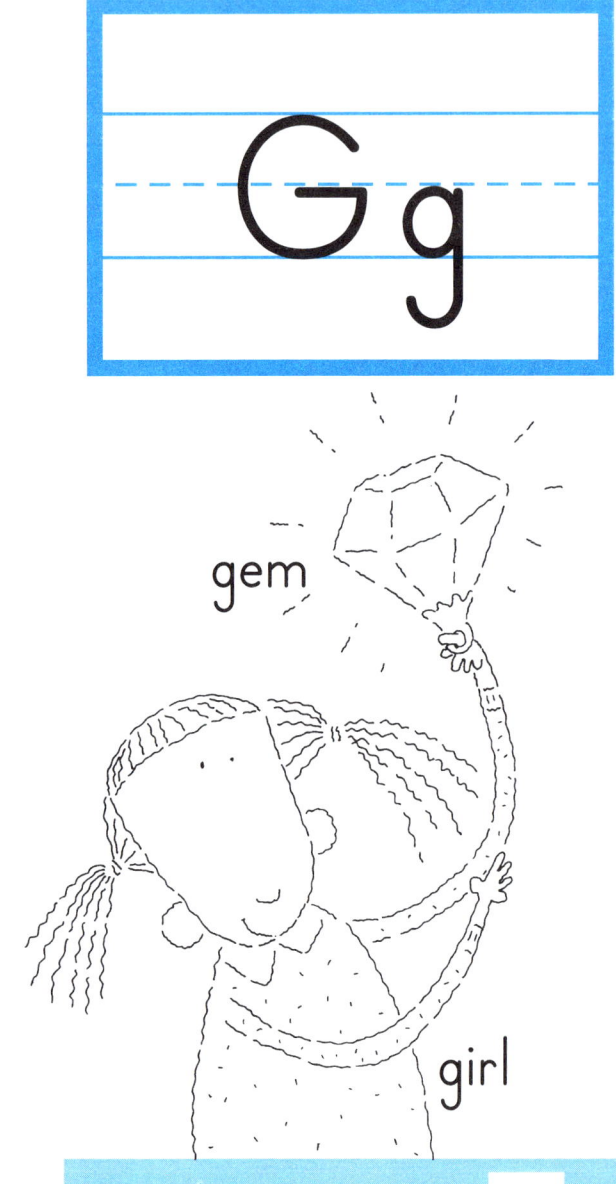

My Words and Pictures

Gg

gem

girl

Aa Bb Cc Dd Ee Ff Gg Hh Ii Jj Kk Ll Mm Nn Oo Pp Qq Rr Ss Tt Uu Vv Ww Xx Yy Zz

© Great Source. All rights reserved.

good

going

get

# My Words and Pictures

Hh

house

hat

Aa Bb Cc Dd Ee Ff Gg Hh Ii Jj Kk Ll Mm Nn Oo Pp Qq Rr Ss Tt Uu Vv Ww Xx Yy Zz

© Great Source. All rights reserved.

happy

her

him

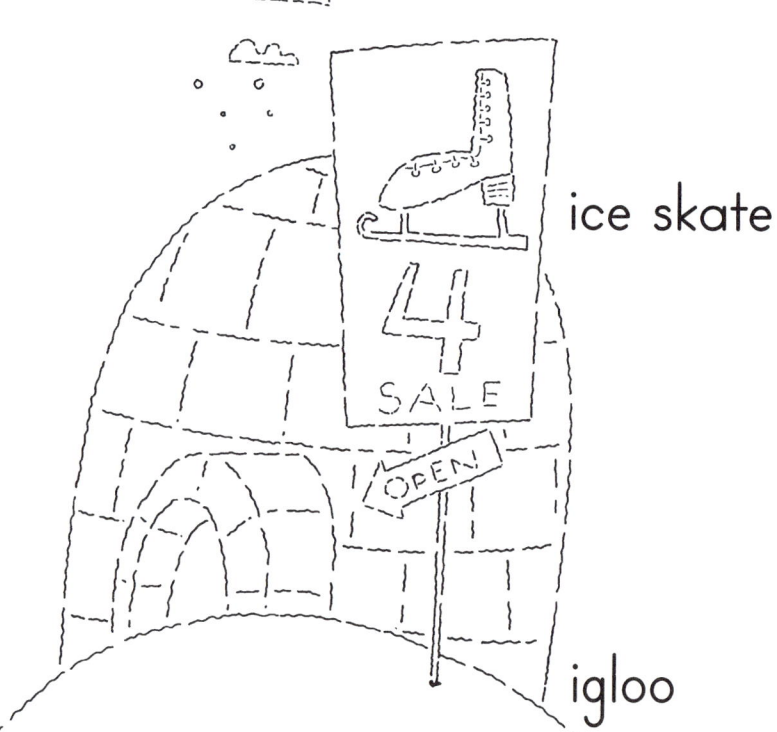

104

My Words and Pictures

I i

ice skate

igloo

Aa Bb Cc Dd Ee Ff Gg Hh Ii Jj Kk Ll Mm Nn Oo Pp Qq Rr Ss Tt Uu Vv Ww Xx Yy Zz

© Great Source. All rights reserved.

is

into

I

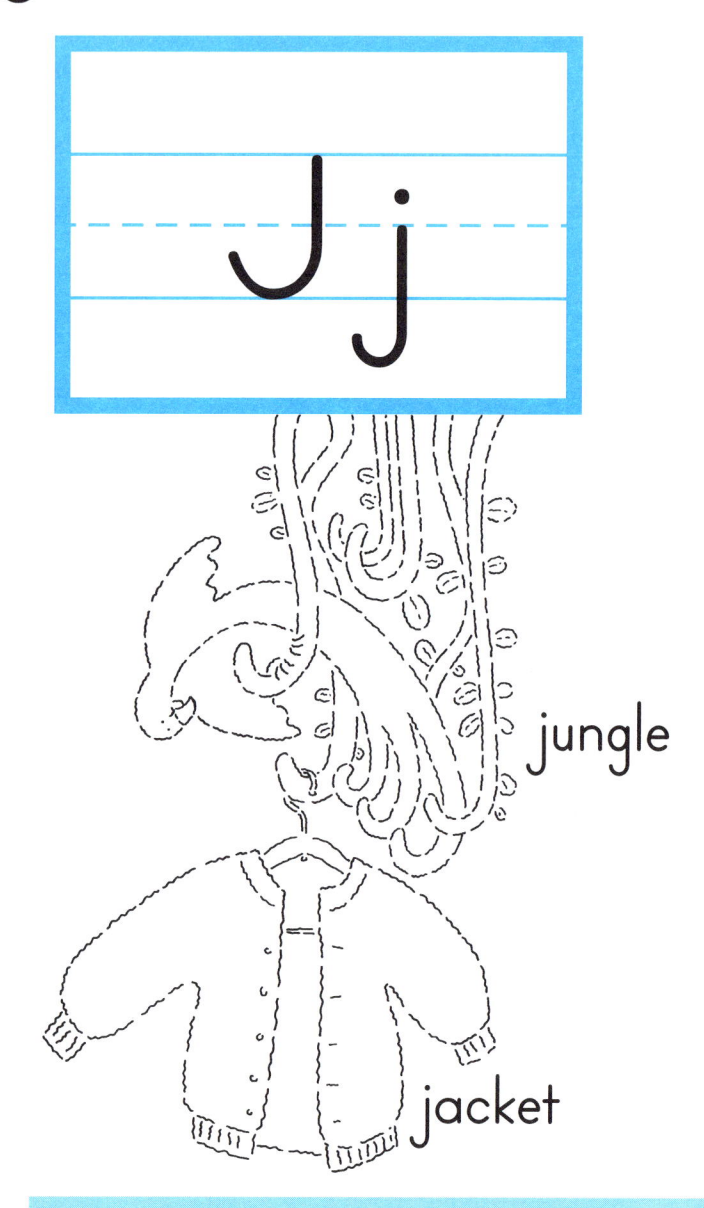

My Words and Pictures

Jj

jungle

jacket

Aa Bb Cc Dd Ee Ff Gg Hh Ii Jj Kk Ll Mm Nn Oo Pp Qq Rr Ss Tt Uu Vv Ww Xx Yy Zz

© Great Source. All rights reserved.

jelly

job

juice

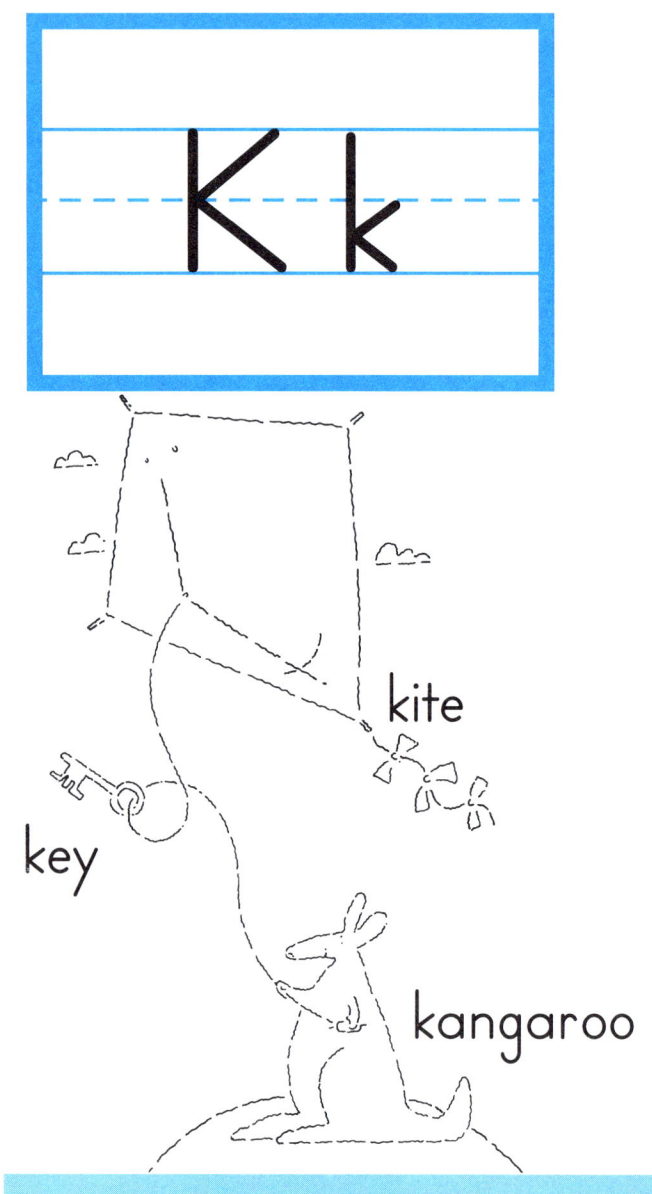

My Words and Pictures

Kk

kite

key

kangaroo

Aa Bb Cc Dd Ee Ff Gg Hh Ii Jj Kk Ll Mm Nn Oo Pp Qq Rr Ss Tt Uu Vv Ww Xx Yy Zz

© Great Source. All rights reserved.

keep

kid

know

110

My Words and Pictures

Ll

leaf

ladybug

Aa Bb Cc Dd Ee Ff Gg Hh Ii Jj Kk Ll Mm Nn Oo Pp Qq Rr Ss Tt Uu Vv Ww Xx Yy Zz

© Great Source. All rights reserved.

little

love

laugh

112

Mm

My Words and Pictures

mouse

MILK

milk

Aa Bb Cc Dd Ee Ff Gg Hh Ii Jj Kk Ll Mm Nn Oo Pp Qq Rr Ss Tt Uu Vv Ww Xx Yy Zz

© Great Source. All rights reserved.

many

more

mother

My Words and Pictures

Nn

night

nest

Aa Bb Cc Dd Ee Ff Gg Hh Ii Jj Kk Ll Mm Nn Oo Pp Qq Rr Ss Tt Uu Vv Ww Xx Yy Zz

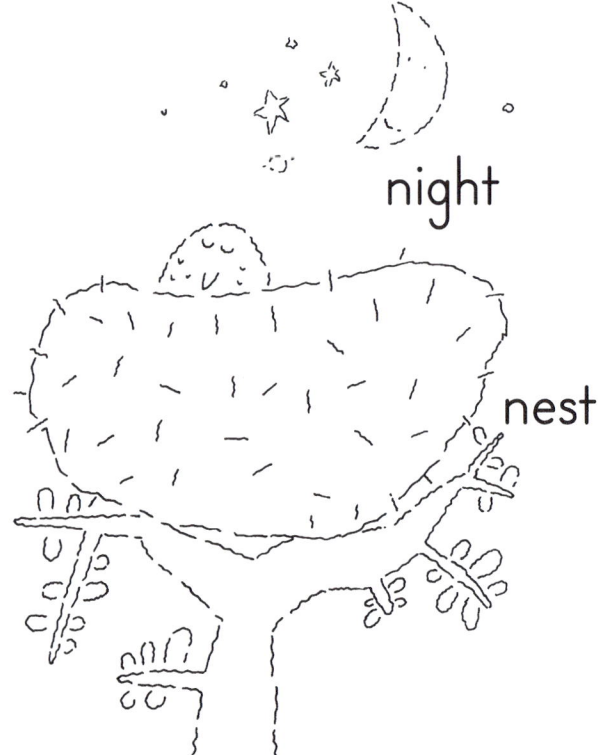

© Great Source. All rights reserved.

name

new

neighbor

My Words and Pictures

Oo

octopus

oak leaf

Aa Bb Cc Dd Ee Ff Gg Hh Ii Jj Kk Ll Mm Nn Oo Pp Qq Rr Ss Tt Uu Vv Ww Xx Yy Zz

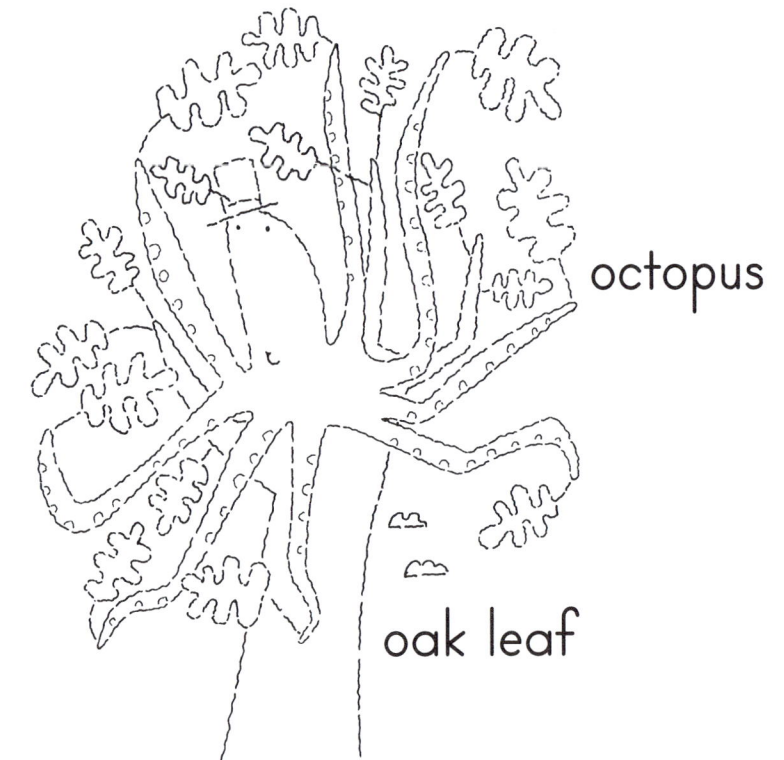

of

our

only

ns and Pictures

Pp

penguin

Aa Bb Cc Dd Ee Ff Gg Hh Ii Jj Kk Ll Mm Nn Oo Pp Qq Rr Ss Tt Uu Vv Ww Xx Yy Zz

© Great Source. All rights reserved.

play

put

people

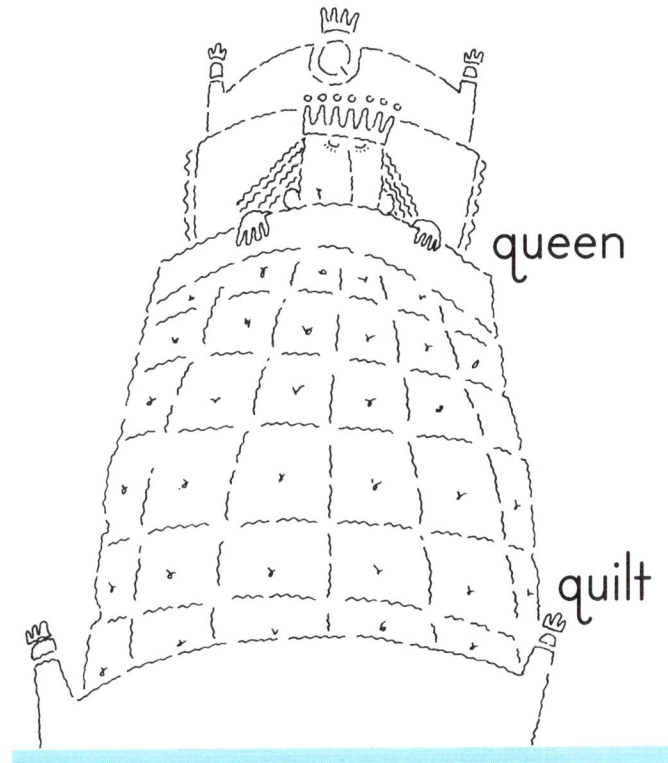

My Words and Pictures

Qq

queen

quilt

Aa Bb Cc Dd Ee Ff Gg Hh Ii Jj Kk Ll Mm Nn Oo Pp Qq Rr Ss Tt Uu Vv Ww Xx Yy Zz

quiet

quarter

quiz

122

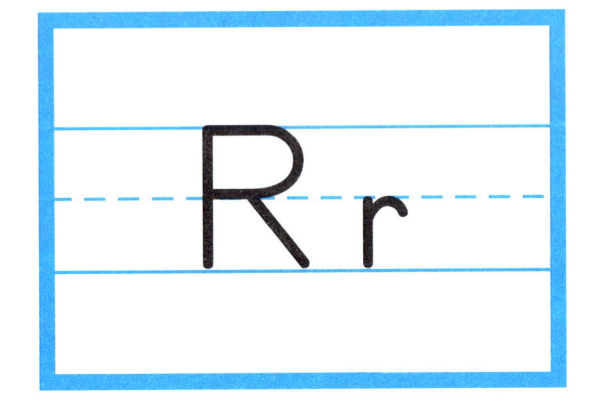

My Words and Pictures

R r

rocket

rabbit

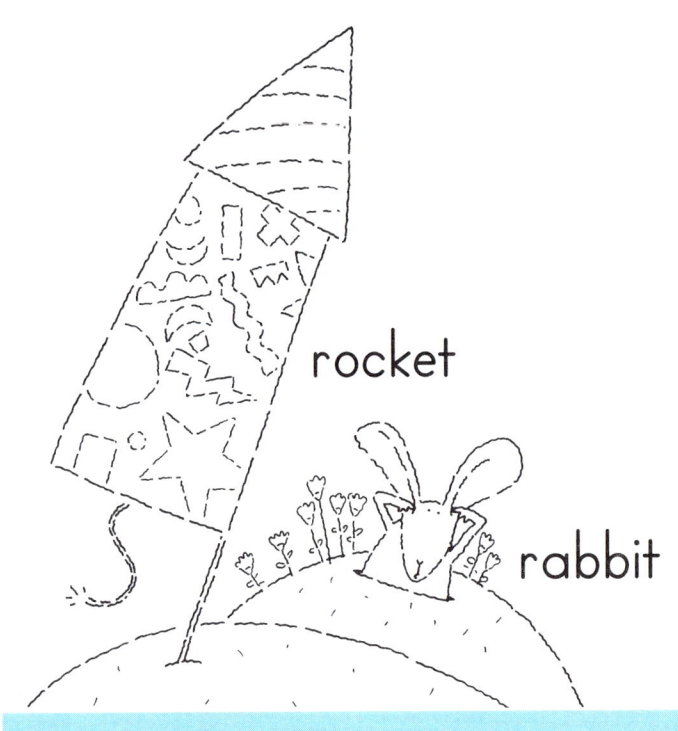

Aa Bb Cc Dd Ee Ff Gg Hh Ii Jj Kk Ll Mm Nn Oo Pp Qq Rr Ss Tt Uu Vv Ww Xx Yy Zz

© Great Source. All rights reserved.

rain

road

room

124

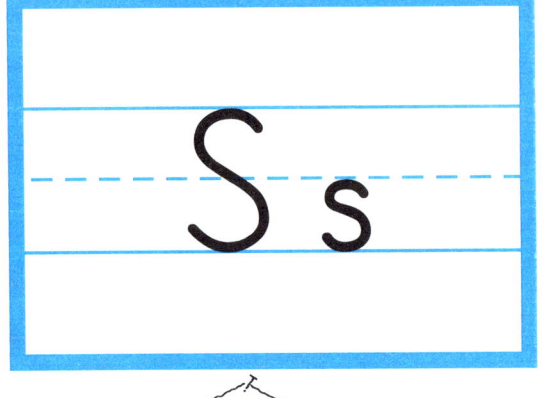

My Words and Pictures

Ss

sailboat
sun
socks

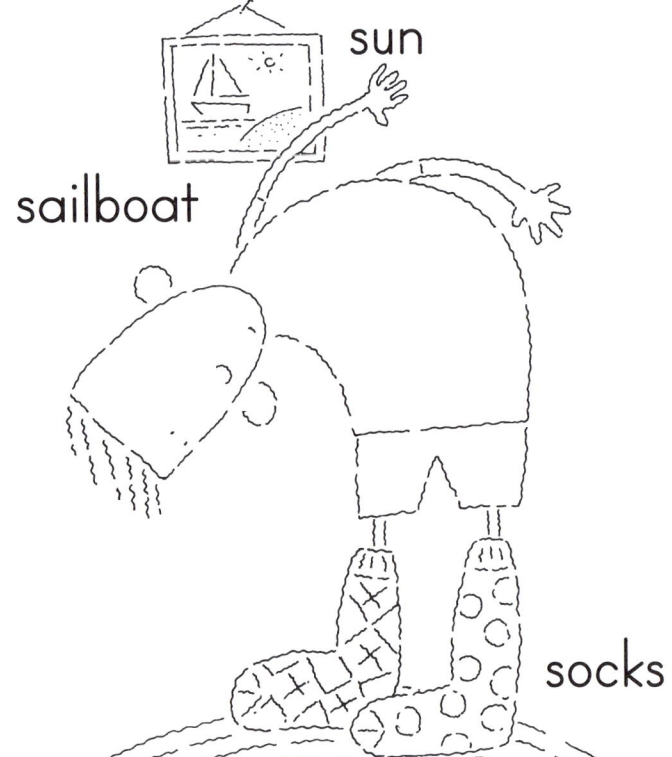

Aa Bb Cc Dd Ee Ff Gg Hh Ii Jj Kk Ll Mm Nn Oo Pp Qq Rr Ss Tt Uu Vv Ww Xx Yy Zz

© Great Source. All rights reserved.

say

sister

saw

My Words and Pictures

Tt

turtle

table

Aa Bb Cc Dd Ee Ff Gg Hh Ii Jj Kk Ll Mm Nn Oo Pp Qq Rr Ss Tt Uu Vv Ww Xx Yy Zz

© Great Source. All rights reserved.

talk

today

they

128

My Words and Pictures

Uu

umbrella

unicycle

Aa Bb Cc Dd Ee Ff Gg Hh Ii Jj Kk Ll Mm Nn Oo Pp Qq Rr Ss Tt Uu Vv Ww Xx Yy Zz

© Great Source. All rights reserved.

under

us

upon

My Words and Pictures

Vv

vase

Aa Bb Cc Dd Ee Ff Gg Hh Ii Jj Kk Ll Mm Nn Oo Pp Qq Rr Ss Tt Uu Vv Ww Xx Yy Zz

© Great Source. All rights reserved.

very

visit

voice

My Words and Pictures

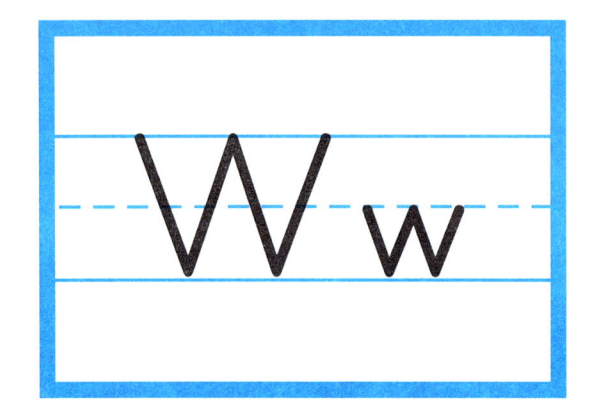

Ww

worm

wheel

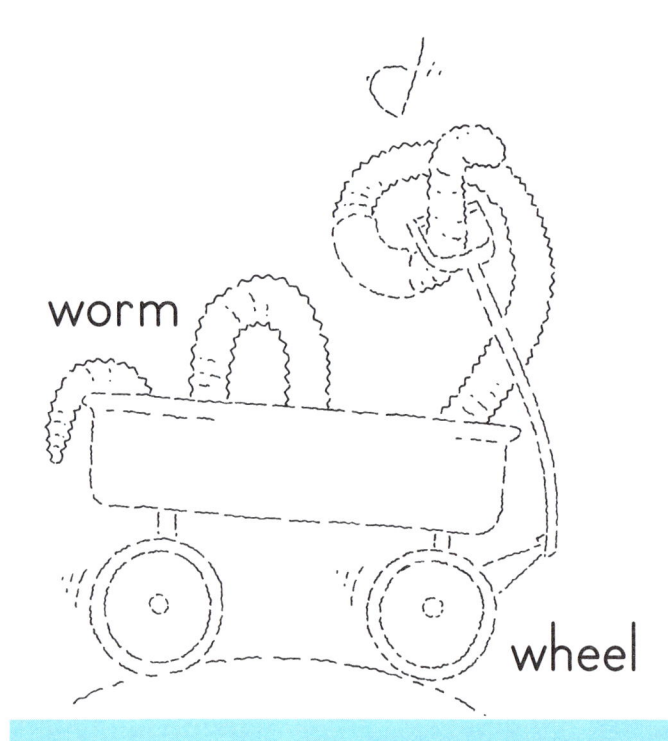

Aa Bb Cc Dd Ee Ff Gg Hh Ii Jj Kk Ll Mm Nn Oo Pp Qq Rr Ss Tt Uu Vv Ww Xx Yy Zz

© Great Source. All rights reserved.

walk

way

woman

My Words and Pictures

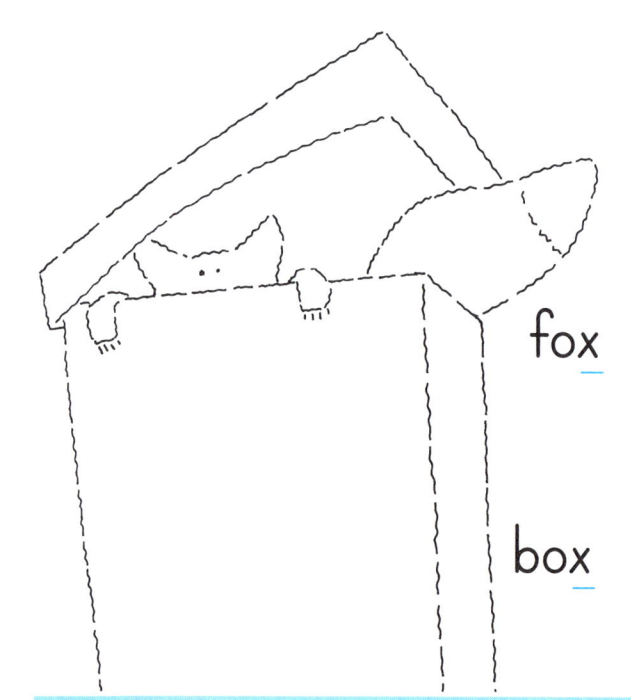

Xx

fox

box

Aa Bb Cc Dd Ee Ff Gg Hh Ii Jj Kk Ll Mm Nn Oo Pp Qq Rr Ss Tt Uu Vv Ww Xx Yy Zz

135

x-ray

fix

six

Handbook Page 121

136

My Words and Pictures

Yy

yarn

Aa Bb Cc Dd Ee Ff Gg Hh Ii Jj Kk Ll Mm Nn Oo Pp Qq Rr Ss Tt Uu Vv Ww Xx Yy Zz

© Great Source. All rights reserved.

137

yes

year

you

My Words and Pictures

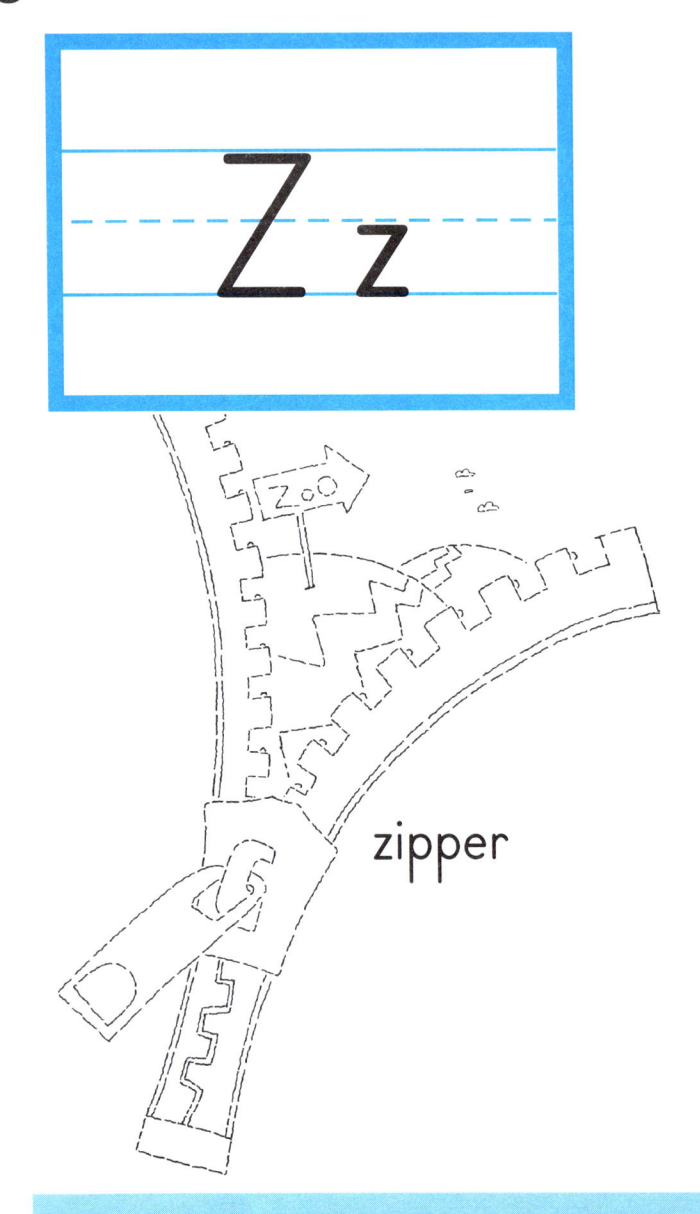

Zz

zipper

Aa Bb Cc Dd Ee Ff Gg Hh Ii Jj Kk Ll Mm Nn Oo Pp Qq Rr Ss Tt Uu Vv Ww Xx Yy Zz

zebra

zigzag

zero

Alphabet Poem

Alligator sits,
Butterfly flits.
Cup of tea,
Duck at sea.
Eggs to cook,
Fish in a brook.
Girl named Mary,
Hat for Harry.
Igloo white,
Jacket bright.
Kite in the sky,
Ladybug shy.
Mouse near a hole,
Nest like a bowl.
Octopus below,
Penguin in the snow.
Quilt for a bed,
Rocket that's red.
Socks for running,
Turtle goes sunning.
Umbrella for showers,
Vase full of flowers.
Wagon to pull,
Box full of wool.
Yarn soft and blue,
Zipper–dee–do!

Write some alphabet words. Draw pictures to go with your words.

We hope you had fun writing in your SkillsBook. Keep writing!

—Your Book Friends